ACTA UNIVERSITATIS GOTHOBURGENSIS

GOTHENBURG STUDIES IN ENGLISH 44

STUDIES OF ERROR GRAVITY

NATIVE REACTIONS TO ERRORS PRODUCED BY SWEDISH LEARNERS OF ENGLISH

BY

STIG JOHANSSON

ACTA UNIVERSITATIS GOTHOBURGENSIS

GÖTEBORG SWEDEN

ISBN 91-7346-054-0
ISSN 0072-503X

Distributors:
ACTA UNIVERSITATIS GOTHOBURGENSIS
Box 5096
S-402 22 Göteborg 5

Printed in Sweden by Minab, Surte 1978

Preface

This investigation continues the work reported earlier in my Papers in Contrastive Linguistics and Language Testing (Lund: Liber/C.W.K. Gleerup, 1975). It has been carried out within the framework of the project Fackspråk och kommunikationseffektivitet, initiated by Professor Alvar Ellegård, Department of English, Gothenburg University, and financed by Statens Humanistiska Forskningsråd. The project started in 1975 and was planned to last for two years. Due to personal reasons, I must leave the project after one year and therefore present a final report at this time. This means that some of the work projected has not been completed and that other parts have not been treated as fully as might have been desirable.

I am grateful to the large numbers of volunteers who have participated in the experiments and to the many others who have assisted me in my work. These include the staff at the University of Lancaster (England) and secondary schools in Lancaster, Preston (England) and Lund (Sweden), who have been very helpful in providing me with opportunities to find volunteers and with facilities for testing. I am also indebted to fil kand Moira Linnarud, Department of English, Lund University, for assistance in carrying out Experiment II (Chapters 3 and 7), to civ ing Rolf Carlsson and civ ing Björn Granström, Royal Institute of Technology, Stockholm, for preparing part of the material used in Experiment V (Chapter 5), and to docent Horst Löfgren, Department of Educational Research, Lund University, for advice on statistics. Thanks are further due to my co-workers within the project, especially fil lic Christina Stendahl, Department of English, Gothenburg University.

There are, to be sure, some persons whose attention is abnormally fixed upon the words rather than upon the topic under discussion, and they sometimes make a nuisance of themselves by pointing out the error and getting it laughed at or recorded before the business in hand is allowed to proceed. One should be kind to these people; they are either fools or linguists!

- Edgar H Sturtevant (1947)

The first step in applying our best scientific knowledge to language problems is to realize that no man's speech is inferior, only different... Our problem is to teach tolerance of difference and acceptance of a man for what he is, not for how he talks.

- Einar Haugen (1975)

CONTENTS

Preface

1 Introduction

2 Subjective and Objective Measures of Error Gravity

3 Overt vs Covert Errors

4 Types of Grammatical and Lexical Errors

5 Foreign Accent and Speech Distortion: Another Look

6 Types of Phonological Errors

7 Native vs Non-Native Judges

8 Conclusions, Applications, and Suggestions for Further Research

Bibliography

1 Introduction

1.1 Error analysis and error evaluation

Error analysis is currently a very active field of research. The study of learners' errors is used as a means of revealing what the learner has yet to know. As the analysis will normally reveal a host of deficiencies, it may be difficult to know where to start and what to emphasize in applying the results. This is where error evaluation fits in, i e the study of error gravity (see Fig 1:1).[2]

Most studies in error analysis have not been concerned in detail with how the results should be applied and hence have not tackled the problem of error evaluation. The need to establish error gravity has, however, occasionally been pointed out, e g

> ... a linguistic approach to error analysis should at least attempt to explicate and rationalise the teacher's subjective evaluations... at the present time nothing is known about the relative gravity, from a native speaker's point of view, of errors of pronunciation, of grammar, or of lexis... Research is needed in this field. (James 1972: 76)

> Research into error analysis is vital, since the teacher should know in advance the type and importance of the errors a particular group of pupils would be likely to make... It may happen that the teacher becomes obsessed with insignificant errors to the exclusion of others that are much more important. Guidelines are required to help establish a scale of relevant priorities in error correction. (Robinson 1973: 192)

Although there have been occasional attempts to establish error gravity in a systematic way (see 1.5.1), error evaluation must be considered a largely neglected field of research.

1.2 The identification of errors

The identification of errors presupposes a norm against which the learner's utterances can be judged. As any student of language knows, there is, however, no single standard of correctness but rather a range of regional, social, stylistic etc varieties, each with its own norm (cf Quirk *et al* 1972: 13ff).

Within the varieties usage may, moreover, be more or less established (cf Quirk & Svartvik 1966: 100). The identification of learners' errors is therefore no simple task. To solve the problem we must use a combination of non-linguistic and linguistic criteria.

For various non-linguistic reasons (practical, pedagogical etc) a teaching programme must concentrate on a selection from among the different varieties of the foreign language. The selection varies depending upon the purpose of the course. Most Swedish learners of English are expected to learn English as used by educated southern British speakers and codified in standard handbooks (dictionaries, grammars, manuals of pronunciation and stylistics). Errors can therefore be identified with reference to these sources. As handbooks are usually incomplete and frequently out of date, the identification of errors must sometimes be regarded as provisional. For the purposes of the present investigation, this is no problem. The study of error gravity will reveal whether the identification was correct and thus supplement our knowledge of the use of English among native speakers.

Serious problems of identification arise if the notion of error is widened to include covert as well as overt errors.[3] Weinreich (1953: 53) points out that "poverty of expression in the second language (i e exaggerated concentration on high-frequency forms and a propensity for circumlocution of difficult forms) is as a rule not recorded as a lack of proficiency, even though it is a result of interference". Such "covert errors" can only be identified if the total performance of the learner is compared with the performance of native speakers in similar situations. Another way of identifying covert errors is to compare the learner's performance in his native and the foreign language in identical situations (cf Váradi 1973). The meanings expressed in the native language then represent what the learner

Fig 1:1 Error analysis and error evaluation

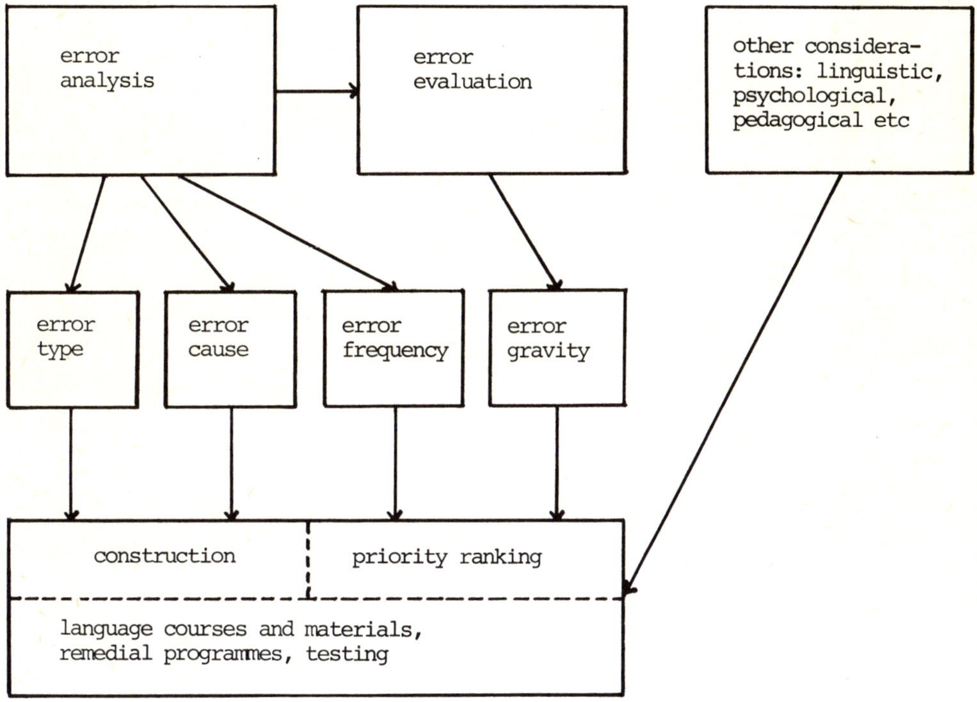

wanted to say, which can be compared with the actual meanings of his foreign-language utterances. The gap between the languages can then be related to an incomplete command of particular aspects of the foreign language.

1.3 Principles of evaluation

Due to the problems of identifying covert errors, most schemes of error evaluation consider overt errors only. The present investigation concentrates on overt errors but also attempts to establish their relative importance as compared with covert errors (see Chapter 3). For the time being, we shall, however, only consider overt errors.

After the identification of errors has been completed, the important task remains to establish a scale of errors. Such a scale could no doubt be founded on purely linguistic criteria, e g whether the error is an infringement of a higher- or lower-level rule,[4] but it seems more relevant to relate the scale to the learner's communicative needs. The more the error interferes with communication, the more serious it seems from the point of view of the learner.[5]

A system of evaluation based on the communicative effect of errors has been outlined in Johansson (1975a: 22ff). According to this system, the first question which should be asked in evaluating an error is whether the erroneous utterance is fully comprehensible or not (see Fig 1:2). If it is not, it is considered a more serious error. If the erroneous utterance is fully comprehensible, it could nevertheless have serious consequences from the point of view of communication, e g make the receiver tired or irritated or draw away his attention from the contents of the message. The further question must therefore be asked whether an error causes irritation or not. Erroneous utterances which are fully comprehensible and cause no irritation constitute the lowest grade of error.

Fig 1:2 The evaluation of errors

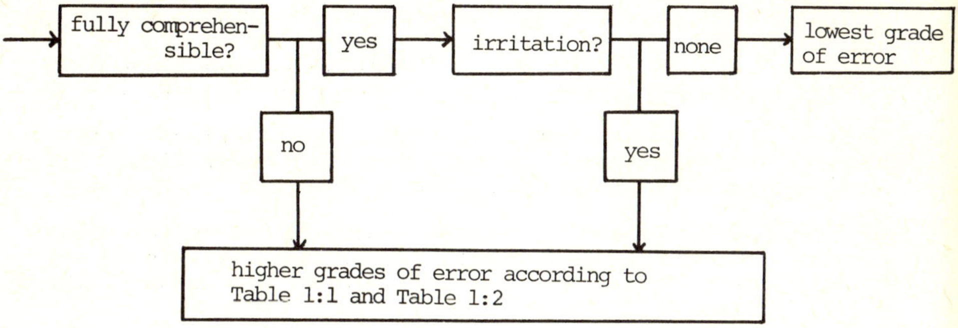

Table 1:1 A hierarchy of errors

Degree of comprehensibility	Frequency	Generality	Score
low	high	high	111
low	high	low	110
low	low	high	101
low	low	low	100
high	low	high	001
high	low	low	000
high	high	high	011
high	high	low	010

Table 1:2 A hierarchy of errors

Degree of irritation	Frequency	Generality	Score
high	high	high	111
high	high	low	110
high	low	high	101
high	low	low	100
low	low	high	001
low	low	low	000
low	high	high	011
low	high	low	010

The suggestion that communicative efficiency should be a basic principle of error evaluation is of course not new but has often been expressed during the last few years, e g[6]

> Fehler..., welche die Zeichen und damit den beabsichten Sinn verändern oder verunklären, sind schwer. (Leisi 1972: 34)

> Wo immer die Kommunikation zusammenbricht und falsche Informationen vermittelt werden, handelt es sich von der linguistischen Seite her um einen schweren Fehler. (Nickel 1972: 20)

> The worst mistakes are those that interfere most with comprehension and communication, while unimportant mistakes do not greatly interfere with communication. (Burt & Kiparsky 1972: 5)

> The grading of errors on a scale should, in other words, be done according to the degree in which each error actually interferes with communication. (Enkvist 1973: 19)

What is new is the insistence that communicative efficiency does not mean comprehensibility in the strict sense. Speech can be severely distorted and yet be intelligible, as is shown by numerous experiments (cf Licklider & Miller 1951). The same applies to written language, as demonstrated by the ability of readers to fill in missing words in cloze tests or interpret idiosyncratic handwriting. But "a reader who must pay close attention to the letters will have difficulty in extracting information from written texts" (Ahlgren 1975: 82). To be communicatively effective, the message must get across swiftly and unambiguously and without undue demands upon the receiver. Hence, the scheme of evaluation presented above includes both comprehensibility and degree of irritation.

For errors which affect comprehensibility or cause irritation, there is a need to determine degrees of comprehensibility and irritation. In order to establish a more detailed hierarchy of errors, it is also possible to introduce further principles of evaluation (see Tables 1:1 and 1:2).[7] The additional principles taken up here, generality and frequency, are old-established ones in systems of error evaluation (cf Johansson 1975a: 22ff). Though more linguistic in nature, these principles are nevertheless closely connected with communicative needs. An error involving a general rule reveals a weakness that may affect an indefinite number of cases and may therefore have more serious consequences for communication than errors involving individual items (words or grammatical exceptions). Likewise, an error involving frequent words or constructions may affect a larger number of cases in actual communication.

The relative importance of these principles of evaluation may not be the same for all kinds of learners but varies depending upon such factors as the goal of the studies and the stage of learning (cf Johansson 1975a: 22ff). The communicative principle may, for example, be more important at earlier stages of learning and with limited-purpose courses. Hence, there are general pedagogical, psychological etc principles which must be taken into account in applying the scheme of evaluation (cf Fig 1:1, "other considerations"). This is especially true if the scale is used as a basis for a marking system in language testing (cf the pedagogical and psychological considerations taken up by Leisi 1972 and Nickel 1972, 1973). It is also important to consider whether observed deviations are systematic errors or occasional lapses (cf Corder 1973: 259), though such a distinction is often difficult to make. The distinction is, however, partly provided for by the "error frequency" box in Fig 1:1. The present investigation will not take up such aspects but will concentrate on the previously neglected area of establishing the communicative effect of errors.

1.4 Topics of research

According to the preceding section, we need to establish the communicative effect of different types of errors. This could be done by submitting samples of errors committed by foreign learners to groups of native speakers. A ranking of error types according to this criterion is in itself an enormous task. However, error type is only one relevant factor. We must also consider that there may be differences depending upon such factors as:

(1) receiver characteristics (e g the receiver's age, education, regional and social dialect, degree of association with foreigners)[8]

(2) the type of language situation (formal or informal, speech or writing, disturbed or undisturbed communication etc)

(3) the role of the sender (whether the foreigner is a tourist, a visiting scientist, a secretary, an interpreter etc)

All of these matters deserve detailed investigation. In particular, it seems relevant to examine the importance of the foreigner role(s). Corder (1973: 47) points out that the foreigner role "has certain expectations associated with it, very often a great tolerance of deviation from the various norms of behaviour, both linguistic and non-linguistic."[9] Later in the same work Corder (1973: 282) says, however, that we do not yet have "a sociological account of the role of foreigners or any hard facts about attitudes to, or expectations of, foreigners' linguistic behaviour in our own or anyone else's culture." The study of error gravity could be an important contribution to our knowledge of these matters.

So far, attention has been focused on how errors produced by second language learners affect the receiver. However, the learner is also a receiver, so it seems relevant in addition to investigate which weaknesses in the learner have the most serious consequences for his perception and comprehension of others. Finally, an exhaustive study should include covert as well as overt errors (cf 1.2, the end). Instead of asking how communication is affected by overt deviance, we must then widen the question and ask how variations in learner language in general affect communication.

1.5 Previous research

As already pointed out, few attempts have been made to establish the communicative effect of errors in a systematic way. We shall review the studies which do exist. In addition, we shall briefly survey some areas of research which are related to or may have implications for the study of error gravity. This survey is necessarily incomplete. Though there is some overlap between the sub-sections, an attempt is made to treat related studies in the same context.

1.5.1 Studies of the communicative effect of learners' errors

Bansal (1965/66, 1969) presented recordings in English by 24 Indian speakers and a control group of 4 RP speakers to groups of listeners of different nationalities. The recordings included connected speech as well as isolated words and sentences. The listeners were native speakers of English (Englishmen and Americans), speakers of English as a second language (Indians and Nigerians) and speakers of English as a foreign language (a group of Germans). The listeners were asked to repeat every word of what they had heard and understood. The results showed a clear difference in intelligibility between Indian and RP speakers as well as wide differences in intelligibility between individual Indian speakers. The difference between the more intelligible and the less intelligible Indians did not lie in any marked differences in their phonemic system but "rather in the frequency of mistakes Indian speakers make in the distribution of vowels and consonants and in patterns of word stress, sentence stress, rhythm and intonation" (Bansal 1969: 171). The British, American and Indian listeners understood the Indian speakers equally well, but the scores were considerably lower for the Nigerian and German groups.

In Engh (1971) groups of German school children were asked to interpret German sentences produced by Swedish school children of the same age. The Germans received a written questionnaire containing 48 isolated sentences which represented different types of lexical and grammatical deviance. They were asked to re-write the sentences ("sie so zu verbessern oder umzuschreiben, dass ein sinnvolles und gut verständliches Deutsch entsteht"). The results indicate that a wrong choice of words very easily gives rise to misinterpretation, whereas there are no or minor difficulties in interpreting sentences containing grammatical errors in subject-verb concord, gender of nouns, case after preposition, etc.

Olsson (1972, 1973) selected 36 deviant English utterances spoken by Swedish pupils in a test of passive formation. The material included 27 examples of "syntactic" errors (e g He were told to work more by his teacher, It been bought by the lady) and 9 examples of "semantic" errors (e g He tell to work more by his teacher, It was buying by the lady). The material was presented orally to groups of native English students in an experiment consisting of an operation test (in the sense of Quirk & Svartvik 1966) and an interpretation test. In the former they were asked to make the sentences negative, interrogative, or replace the subject by another word. In the following interpretation test they were told to correct the sentences. The most important results were that the intelligibility scores were very high in general but that the "semantic" errors were found to block communication to a higher degree than did the "syntactic" errors.

The studies by Bansal, Engh and Olsson tested intelligibility by having (usually) native speakers reproduce or re-write sentences containing learners' errors. There are also investigations where native speakers have been asked to give judgements of material produced by foreign learners.[10]

In Dimitrijević & Djordjević (1971) a comparison is made between the assessment of Yugoslav university students' English pronunciation by four groups of judges (3 categories of Yugoslav judges as well as 5 native speakers of English). The test consisted of recordings of isolated sentences and a passage. Each test item was judged on a five-point scale ranging from "perfect pronunciation, equal to the native speakers" to "quite bad, not understandable or acceptable". The native English evaluators showed the greatest similarity in judgement. A remarkable result is also that the natives were more tolerant in the assessment of individual sounds than were the other groups but less so in the assessment of stress and intonation as evidenced by the low marks given for the continuous text.

Stenström (1975) submitted 316 grammatically incorrect English sentences or parts of sentences, produced by Swedish teacher trainees, for judgement to a group of 4 native speakers of English. The test items, which were presented in written form and out of context, were judged on a four-point scale (0: "uncertain", 1: "acceptable in colloquial and careless language", 2: "wrong but comprehensible", 3: "wrong and incomprehensible"). The great majority (251) were judged to be "wrong but comprehensible", while very few (27) were evaluated as "wrong and incomprehensible". Among the former were test items containing errors in verb form, article errors, concord errors, etc. Items judged to be "wrong and incomprehensible" varied in kind but were often those where understanding was obscured by lack of context.

Linnarud (1975) contains a comparison of judgements made by a native speaker of English with no academic training and an academically trained evaluator. The material consisted of 36 English essays written by Swedish university students. Judgements, which were made on a three-point scale (1: "poor", 2: "average", 3: "good"), showed a sensitivity to covert as well as overt errors. Essays with a lower lexical density and/or variation normally received a lower grade than those with a higher proportion of content words and/or greater variation of vocabulary. The judge with no academic training was somewhat more generous in his judgement than was the academically trained evaluator. In particular, the untrained evaluator seemed to be more lenient towards essays containing overt errors.

In some investigations judgement tests have been combined with intelligibility tests or other measures of communicative efficiency. This applies especially to the studies in Johansson (1975a: 34ff), which have been summarized in Section 2.2. Another investigation which included both judgement and comprehension tests is Juhász (1970: 49ff). Juhász gave a series of tests to native speakers of German (school children and university students). The material consisted of 7 correct and 34 incorrect German sentences produced in a translation test by Hungarian pupils. Each incorrect sentence contained an interference error (grammatical or lexical). The sentences included were such as an educated native speaker of German would be expected to understand in spite of the error (Juhász 1970: 49). The subjects were given a judgement test and two operation tests. In the judgement test they listened to the sentences read by the experimenter and were asked to judge each item on a five-point scale (1: correct, 2: incorrect, 3: doubtful, 4: incomprehensible, 5: not incorrect, but another way of expression is preferable). In a following operation test they listened to the material again and were asked to re-write the sentences which they had previously given the grades 2 or 5. In the last operation test they heard the sentences once more and the task was to re-write all the items which had received the grades 1, 3 or 5 in as many ways as possible. Though Juhász was mainly interested in establishing whether the test sentences were correct or incorrect (and had deliberately included material that was expected to be comprehensible, cf above), the results are nevertheless interesting from our point of view. The grade 4 (incomprehensible) was used only in 1.84 per cent of the responses. Moreover, test sentences were normally interpreted in the intended sense in the operation tests.

The studies taken up so far have mainly been concerned with reactions to different error types: segmental vs prosodic errors, grammatical vs lexical errors, overt vs covert errors, etc. Most of the investigations have used university students or school children as test subjects, but the type of receiver was varied in some cases (Bansal 1965/66, 1969, Dimitrijević & Djordjević 1971, Linnarud 1975, Johansson 1975a). Of the other factors mentioned in Section 1.4, the foreigner role has not been taken into account at all and the type of language situation has only received marginal attention (Johansson 1975a). There are, however, two studies which concentrate on different aspects of the language situation, i e Chaiklin (1955) and Lane (1963).

Chaiklin (1955) is an attempt to investigate native American listeners' adaptation in understanding speakers with foreign dialect. Two Slovakian speakers recorded 4 intelligibility lists and 3 short prose passages in English. A test tape was constructed for each speaker consisting of intelligibility lists alternating with prose passages. Two 10-member panels of American college students listened to one test tape each on two occasions. They responded to the intelligibility lists by writing down the responses heard on prepared answer forms but were not required to make any responses while listening to the passages of connected discourse. Mean intelligibility scores were computed for each list during the two testing occasions. The results showed changes in the level of response between the lists and considerable variability between individual listeners. The changes observed appeared, however, to "have little consistency, which leads to the conclusion that for the time periods tested in this experiment there are probably no stable adaptation effects produced in the understanding of speakers with a foreign dialect" (Chaiklin 1955: 169f).

Lane (1963) reports two experiments examining reactions to foreign accent under conditions of masking and filtering. Twenty-four American undergraduates listened to recorded articulation lists rendered by one American and three foreign-born speakers who had a strong foreign accent according to listener ratings. The native languages of the foreign speakers were Punjabi, Serbian and Japanese. The listeners were told that they would hear common English monosyllables and that they were to write them down. Mean intelligibility scores were calculated for eight conditions of masking and filtering. Reducing the speech to noise ratio to -5 dB or the transmission bandwidth to 500 cps yielded approximately 50% reduction in intelligibility for both native and foreign-accent speech. The latter was approximately 40% less intelligible than native speech under all experimental conditions. Individual differences among the foreign speakers had no marked effect on intelligibility scores. It is also of interest to note that there was no appreciable interaction effect due to the combination of the two types of distortion (i e foreign accent and masking/filtering).

In conclusion, we shall take up a study which varied both aspects of the language situation (such as those examined by Chaiklin and Lane) and the category of receivers. Brodkey (1972) gave dictation tests consisting of extracts from lectures by two Anglo-American college lecturers and interviews with four foreign speakers of English. The foreigners were two speakers of Spanish-accented English as well as a Vietnamese and an Indian, though the latter were eliminated as they were unintelligible to listeners more than 50% of the time. Some of the recordings had a noticeable background hum, while others were undistorted. The listeners, who were asked to write down everything they heard word by word, were Anglo-American and American Indian college students, foreign university students and Anglo-American teachers (some of them with experience in teaching English as a second language). Information was collected on personal data such as age, sex, Spanish-English bilingualism, etc for the listener groups. Some of the speakers were known in advance to some of the listeners. The results indicated that prior listener-experience with the voice of the speaker is a prominent factor in intelligibility, which means that accommodation to the speaker over time is a crucial variable.[11] A combination of increasing age, education and experience in teaching

English as a second language seems to increase ability to comprehend unfamiliar speakers. Bilingual Spanish-English listeners have an advantage in decoding Spanish-accented English, while American Indians scored below the foreign university students (which were otherwise the lowest-scoring group) in ability to decode a heavy Spanish accent. Neither the clear nor the noise-contaminated tape showed consistent superiority in maximizing discrimination among listener groups, though the unclear tapes received consistently lower scores.

1.5.2 Accentedness studies

A large number of investigations have dealt with evaluational reactions to accents within one language. Labov (1966) played recordings of American English speakers and asked listeners to assign the speakers to the occupations for which their speech was most suited. The results revealed very consistent differentiations among the listeners. Many accentedness studies have used the "matched-guise" technique, where listeners judge characteristics of a speaker who reads the same passage in two or more dialects (e g Canadian and Parisian style French in Preston, 1963, Yorkshire and London accented English in Strongman & Woosley, 1967) or languages (e g French and English in Lambert _et al_, 1960). The listeners are kept unaware that they are hearing the same speaker in different guises and are instead set to hear a series of different persons. Investigations of this kind have revealed interesting correlations between the speaker's language or dialect and listener judgements of the speaker's personality, social status, etc.

Accentedness studies such as those referred to have been criticized because of the artificiality of the experimental situation, statistical weaknesses, etc (Lee 1971). Nevertheless, we shall take up two investigations using varieties of the matched guise technique applied to foreign accents, i e Giles (1970) and Landén & Trankell (1975).

Giles (1970) used recordings of one male speaker reading the same English passage with 13 different foreign and regional accents. 177 subjects (selected according to a 2x2x2x2 matrix of age, sex, social class and geographical region) listened to the recordings and were asked to identify each accent and rate it across 3 dimensions on 7-point scales. The dimensions were concerned with "how pleasant-unpleasant they thought a particular accent sounded", "how comfortable-uncomfortable they would feel if interacting with the accented speaker concerned", and "how much prestige or status was associated with speaking this accent" (Giles 1970: 215). In a second, "conceptual", task test subjects received lists mentioning 16 accents, 12 of them identical to those represented in the listening task, and were asked to rate these according to the same 3 dimensions as in the listening task. The results indicated that the subjects were able to identify the accents in the listening task, though the success of identification was greater in the older than in the younger group (17-year-olds vs 12-year-olds). The correlations between the rating in the conceptual and the listening task were extremely high. The inter-dimension correlations in both tasks were also very high, which "gives rise to the notion that the scales are best considered as three distinct variants of a single evaluative dimension" (Giles 1970: 224). The factors of age, sex, social class and regional membership were found to be important determinants of evaluation, but a generalized pattern of ranking accents emerged. RP received higher ratings than the other accents represented. French-accented English received very high ratings, whereas other foreign accents, notably Indian and West Indian, scored low. The lowest ratings were, however, given to the Birmingham accent.

Landén & Trankell (1975) made two short interviews with an Indian speaker of Swedish. The interviews dealt with two subjects, the interviewee's opinions on the United States and her reactions to a well-known film. The interviews were transcribed and corrected versions were prepared. These were later recorded by a native Swedish actress. The interviews were played to large groups of Swedish listeners (pupils in their upper teens as well as adults enrolled in a secondary school) on two occasions. On the first occasion they heard one interview in the original version and the other in the corrected version, on the second they listened to the interviews again but with a change of speakers. The listeners were asked to judge each speaker on each occasion across 4 dimensions on 15-point scales. The dimensions were intelligence, power of judgement, degree of culture/education, and emotional maturity (intelligens, omdömesförmåga, bildningsgrad, emotionell mognad). The results showed that both speakers received higher ratings in the film interview and lower ratings in the interview on the United States. The listeners therefore disregarded the foreign accent in making their judgements. The authors conclude that the listener's impression of a speaker is based on the content of what is said rather than on the occurrence of grammatical and phonological errors.

Landén & Trankell's results seem to conflict with the results of a large number of other accentedness studies. However, their study includes an element which was not varied in the latter, i e content. It may very well be that variations in content (cf Lee 1971: 411ff) are the major variable in judging speakers rather than features of expression. Nevertheless, it is necessary to repeat Landén & Trankell's experiment with other speakers and listener groups, before the results can be generalized. Above all, there is a need to measure the listener's comprehension as well as attitude, since a number of the subjects in Landén & Trankell's experiment commented that they had difficulties in understanding the foreign speaker.

1.5.3 Dialect intelligibility testing

Studies of mutual intelligibility between dialects of one language are related to investigations of reactions to foreign accent. An interesting investigation of this kind of research is Kirk (1970), which will be summarized here as it is important from a methodological point of view. Kirk recorded samples of speech in different Mazatec communities and presented them as comprehension tests to speakers in other dialect communities. The listeners were asked to answer comprehension questions (phrased in their own dialect) on the passages. They were also asked to indicate whether it was easy or difficult for them to understand the speech of various other communities. Interestingly enough, there were high correlations between these two measures (cf the discussion of subjective and objective measures of error gravity in Chapter 2).

1.5.4 Studies of reactions to speech defects

There is an extensive literature dealing with speech defects. Though foreign accent (or linguistic foreignism in general) certainly is not what is ordinarily meant by a speech defect, there may be an advantage in considering these deviations together. One aspect which is very prominent in discussions of speech defects is the effect of the deviations on the speaker. Note the definition of defective speech in Van Riper (1947: 15).

> Speech is defective when it deviates so far from the speech of other people that it calls attention to itself, interferes with communication, or causes its possessor to be maladjusted.

The possible effect of deviance on the speaker seems to have been neglected in studies of the communicative effect of learners' errors. A speech pathologist, Chreist (1964: XXX), writes that "many speakers with a foreign accent feel very insecure, even inferior". To combat such feelings of insecurity or inferiority it is useful to have available systematic studies of receiver reactions to learners' errors.

Many studies deal with listener reactions to defective speech. Some of them will be briefly summarized here, as they are of methodological interest. Morrison (1955), after reviewing investigations based on the frequency of error or the like, points out that such measures may be inadequate in specifying articulation defectiveness:

> Because the psychological reactions of a listener probably vary with respect to differing defective sounds and to varying combinations of them, the assumption that a mere enumeration of them would be sufficient seems unreasonable. (Morrison 1955: 348)

Morrison asked naive and sophisticated listeners to rate samples of speech on a nine-point equal-appearing intervals scale of articulation defectiveness. Reliable scale values of severity were obtained in this way. There was high agreement between expert and naive raters, though the "expert observers in general tended to rate the segments somewhat more severly than did the naive observers" (Morrison 1955: 350). The method of equal-appearing intervals, which will be used extensively in this investigation, has been employed in many other studies. In a comparison of four psychological scaling methods Sherman & Moodie (1957: 706) found it to be "the most useful [method] for scaling defectiveness of articulation ". Similar results are reported in Sherman & Silverman (1968).

Jordan (1960), who states that one of the major goals of therapy is "to reduce as quickly as possible and as much as possible those deviations which are distracting to the listener" (Jordan 1960: 303), attempts to establish the relationship between listener ratings and articulation test measures. 22 measures obtained from phonetic analysis of 150 children's articulation test responses were compared with ratings of 30-second speech samples on a nine-point equal-appearing intervals scale by 36 listeners. Among the results could be mentioned (Jordan 1960: 318):

> Reactions of listeners to articulation defectiveness are primarily dependent upon two factors: frequency with which articulatory deviations occur and degree of articulatory deviations.
>
> To the listener, omissions are more deviant than substitutions and substitutions are more deviant than distortions.

Jordan concludes by pointing out that articulation test measures of number of defective items and number of defective single sounds are highly related to listener ratings of articulation defectiveness.

Certain studies compare the ratings of trained and untrained listeners (cf the results in Morrison, 1955, reported above). Perrin (1954) used speech samples from 7 subjects which were rated by an untrained group consisting of 26 university students enrolled in an introductory psychology course and a trained group consisting of 13 students participating in a course in clinical methods in speech correction. The results indicated that trained and untrained judges do not differ significantly in their evaluations of the severity of functional articulation defects. However, the "untrained observers were slightly more in agreement with themselves than were the trained observers" (Perrin 1954: 51). Wilson & Gasek (1975) evaluated whether pre-information influenced experienced and inexperienced speech clinicians' ratings of a child's articulation. 30 experienced clinicians with at least one year of paid professional experience and 30 students of speech pathology who had completed no more than a quarter of practicum therapy experience rated the articulation of 5 children on a nine-point equal-appearing intervals scale. The pre-information consisted of a spurious summary of the child's initial speech evaluation. Results were in the direction of the pre-information for both groups, but "this effect was much stronger in the case of the experienced examiners than in the case of the inexperienced examiners" (Wilson & Gasek 1975: 20).

In conclusion, we shall take up a study where the cloze technique was applied to the study of aphasic speech. Fillenbaum & Jones (1962) made transcripts of the speech of 9 aphasic patients and 3 normal control subjects. Test versions were prepared where every fifth word was deleted. These were administered to groups of university students. The cloze scores were found to discriminate among transcripts from aphasic and control speakers. Fillenbaum & Jones (1962: 189) suggest that "the cloze procedure can provide an overall index of the divergence of a speaker's language from normal".

1.5.5 Acceptability testing

The distinction between acceptable and unacceptable sentences is often problematic and frequently troubles the linguist in describing a language. For this reason, techniques of acceptability testing have been developed. Though there is normally a considerable difference between learners' errors and sentences which the linguist is uncertain about in describing a language, some of these techniques may be applicable in both cases. We shall take up two particular aspects of acceptability testing, i e the relationship between subjective and objective measures of acceptability and the relationship between judgements made by linguistically sophisticated and naive subjects.

In the well-known investigation by Quirk & Svartvik (1966) an attempt is made to develop a more objective testing method than a straightforward judgement test. Quirk & Svartvik propose a method according to which the acceptability of a sentence is indirectly measured by an informant's ability to replicate its form after having performed a simple operation on it. Nevertheless, their study revealed a good correlation between this operation test and a judgement test. The validity of the judgement technique is further demonstrated by the close agreement between judgement results in Quirk & Svartvik and those obtained for similar or identical sentences in Davy & Quirk (1969) and Johansson (1975a: 150ff) as well as by the correspondence between judgement tests and more objective measures in the latter study. It may therefore be sufficient under most circumstances to use the (simpler) judgement technique in investigations of linguistic acceptability.[12]

Many discussions between linguists have shown that there are considerable differences in judgements of acceptability. Spencer (1973) examines possible differences between linguists and non-linguists. 150 sentences from 6 linguists' articles were presented to 43 linguistically naive and 22 linguistically non-naive native speakers of English. Native speakers (naive and non-naive) agreed among themselves as to the acceptability or unacceptability of 80% of the sentences. Subjects shared intuitions with the linguists in only half of the cases. Spencer (1973: 87) suggests that the "linguist views language in a highly specialized way" and that his description "may be an artifactual system which reflects the accretion of conceptual organization by linguists".[13] There is some evidence in Quirk & Svartvik's study that linguistically naive judges may be more consistent in giving judgements of acceptability than non-naive evaluators (Quirk & Svartvik 1966: 32ff). The latter were found to be more adept in carrying out the operations but were more often out of step with their fellows in judging the test sentences. Similar tendencies appeared in Johansson (1975a: 163ff), where a group of linguistics students showed greater success in identifying sentences masked by noise than did a group of non-linguistics students but were also less consistent in some cases in giving acceptability judgements. These results indicate that linguistic sophistication may be an obstacle rather than an advantage in judgements of acceptability.[14]

1.5.6 Psycholinguistic experimentation

A great number of studies deal with how syntactic or semantic characteristics of sentences influence the performance of test subjects in visual and aural perception, reading, learning, memory, etc. Most of these examine relationships between non-deviant sentences of different kinds, but there are also experiments investigating reactions to deviant vs non-deviant sentences or reactions to different types of deviance. Miller <u>et al</u> (1951)

showed that content words were more intelligible when heard in the context of a grammatical sentence than when scrambled and spoken in isolation as items on a list. In later experiments, Miller & Isard (1963) found that grammatical sentences were repeated more correctly than ungrammatical or semantically anomalous sentences. Grammatical sentences have also been shown to be memorized more readily than ungrammatical sentences (Marks & Miller 1964). The studies taken up so far have been concerned with rather gross differences. We shall now look at some experiments which yield more detailed information on reactions to linguistic deviance.

Gladney & Krulee (1967) introduced errors into English sentences in a systematic way in order to study their effect on the performance of test subjects in a sentence repetition task. Errors were introduced in subject, verb or object position by substituting an adjective or adverb for a noun or verb. Sentences were presented with or without prior knowledge of the presence or absence of an error. Subjects viewed slides of one sentence at a time and were able to control viewing time. They were told to continue the exposure until they could repeat the sentence correctly. The experimenter recorded the exposure times for the sentences as well as errors in the responses. In general, the effect of an error was to increase average viewing time. Knowledge of what to expect had no effect on the performance of test subjects. Errors in the verb were more disruptive than errors in either the subject or object position. Incorrect repetitions were infrequent but were consistent with the measure of viewing time, i e they occurred more often with sentences containing an error in the verb. To explain these findings, the authors point out that errors in the subject or object leave the basic sentence structure undisturbed. On the other hand, errors in the verb are more disruptive, as it functions as a marker in outlining the basic syntactic structure of sentences.[15]

Downey & Hakes (1968) studied the effect of violations of three types of syntactic rules: selection restrictions, strict subcatagorization rules, and phrase-structure rules (cf the hierarchy proposed in Chomsky 1965). Test sentences were constructed by substituting an inappropriately marked transitive verb, and intransitive for a transitive verb, or an adjective for a verb in transitive sentences. The sentences were ranked on a scale of acceptability in the order listed above (from less to more deviant). In a free-recall learning task sentences containing violations of phrase-structure rules took longest to learn, but the learning ease of the two remaining types of rule violations was the reverse of that expected (though the differences between the types was not statistically significant). Stolz (1969) reports results which seem to contradict Downey & Hakes' findings in this respect. Subjects rated sentences containing violations of selection restrictions or strict subcategorization rules. The former received higher ratings than the latter and were also recalled significantly better in a free-recall learning task. It should, however, be noted that Downey & Hakes used only verb violations, whereas Stolz included violations of selection restrictions both in noun phrases and verb phrases. Danks & Glucksberg (1970) asked subjects to rate sentences containing inappropriate determiners in noun phrases, sentences containing violations of selection restrictions or subcategorization involving the verb, and completely ungrammatical sentences. The three types of deviance were ranked in the order listed (from less to more deviant). Moore (1972) attempts to separate the factors of violation type and location of the violation which were not distinguished in the two last-mentioned investigations. Test sentences were constructed containing the three types of violations used in the Downey & Hakes (1969) study in three locations: the subject, the verb, and the object. The relationships between the sentences were studied in a speeded recognition task and a rating task. There was a strong correspondence between the two experiments. Though violations of phrase-structure rules were found to be the most deviant, other results indicated that the hierarchy proposed in Chomsky (1965) is not psychologically real. Rather, a subject's "assessment of grammaticality appears to depend upon whether the violation occurs within a S-V-O sequence, or within a subordinate part of the sentence" (Moore 1972: 558), i e violations affecting S-V-O relationships are more deviant than those involving modifiers of subject and object. This conclusion is supported by the results of Krulee & Ramsburg (1974), who investigated three types of anomalies (in the subject phrase, predicate phrase, or the relationship between the subject and the predicate phrase) in three types of sentences (equational, transitive, and intransitive). The technique of Gladney & Krulee (1967) was used in order to study the effect of the deviance (cf above). For all types of sentences, the presence of an anomaly caused an increase in processing time. Among the results could be mentioned that equational sentences were processed more easily than were transitive or intransitive sentences and that errors affecting the "primary proposition" were more disruptive than those affecting "secondary propositions" (anomalies within the subject, object or predicate complement).

The studies presented so far deal with reactions to specific types of syntactic or semantic deviance. More general problems are investigated in Lazerson (1974/75). Caxton's preface to the _Eneydos_ was read in five versions by skilled readers of modern English: the original version which uses highly variable spelling and an archaic syntactic-semantic system, a version with the highly variable spelling retained but with the syntactic-semantic system of modern English, a completely modernized version, a modernized version where the bottom half of every line of print was eradicated, and a modernized version where a line was drawn horizontally through the middle of each line of print. Three experiments were carried out measuring silent reading performance, oral reading performance, and eye movements. The results indicated that highly variable spelling detrimentally affected several measures of reading performance (reading time, comprehension, the number of regressions, etc). Highly variable spelling combined with an archaic syntactic-semantic system caused a further reduction in reading efficiency. On the other hand, a change of the visibility of print did not materially affect the reading efficiency of the skilled reader of modern English.[16] Lazerson (1974/75: 614) concludes that "the skilled reader's performance is more detrimentally affected by a conflict between the marks on the printed page and his knowledge of the language than by a reduction in the amount of featural information provided by the marks on the printed page".

In conclusion, we shall take up a study which investigates strategies of interpreting ungrammatical sentences, viz Shanon (1973).[17] Ungrammatical Hebrew sentences were presented to subjects who were required to interpret them. The sentences contained violations of agreement rules concerning number, gender, number and gender, and tense. In simple cases only one constituent had to be changed in order to form a grammatical sentence; in more complicated cases three changes were necessary. Among the findings were that the verb was normally changed in cases of discord between the subject and the verb. In the more complicated cases the interpretations given were those which required changing the least number of surface constituents to make the sentence grammatical. Other results were that morphologically marked forms showed a resistance to change and that the order of constituents was not relevant.

1.5.7 Cloze test research

Research with cloze tests and other forms of sentence completion tests shows that the degree of redundancy of language is high. Certain studies give information on differences between grammatical classes in tests of this kind. Aborn *et al* (1959) varied the word class of the omitted word, the amount of context and the place of omission in a test based on sentences drawn randomly from popular magazines. They found that the success in completion for words belonging to a given class is, in general, inversely related to the size of the class. Nouns, verbs, adjectives and adverbs received much lower completion scores than did pronouns and other function words. The amount of context and the place of omission were also found to be relevant factors. The results as regards grammatical class are consistent with those of Fillenbaum *et al* (1963), who gave cloze tests with deletion of every second, third, fourth, fifth or sixth word, based on a transcript of running speech. Fillenbaum *et al* studied the success in verbatim identification and form-class identification of the omitted words. Both form-class and verbatim scores were found to increase moderately with decreasing frequency of deletion, but test subjects did fairly well, particularly with form-class identification, even when every second item was deleted. There were differences in completion scores between different grammatical classes, though the differences were small in the case of form-class identification. Verbatim identification was high for pronouns and other function words (articles, auxiliary verbs, prepositions, conjunctions, etc) but much lower for nouns, full verbs, adjectives, and adverbs. There were, however, substantial differences between items within any given grammatical class with regard to both verbatim and form-class completion.

If the preceding studies investigate the relationship between grammatical class and predictability, other studies attempt to determine the contribution to meaning of different grammatical classes. As is to be expected, there is a close agreement between the results of the two types of investigation. Louthan (1965) gave comprehension questions on passages presented in original form or in seven cloze versions. The latter included a version with random deletions and six versions with deletion of items belonging to specific grammatical classes. The rate of deletion was approximately every 10th word. Comprehension scores on passages with random deletion or deletion of nouns, full verbs and adjectives+adverbs were found to be significantly lower than those on the control passages in which the text was unaltered. On the other hand, there were no appreciable differences between the latter and the scores on passages with deletion of prepositions+conjunctions and pronouns, while passages with deletion of noun determiners even produced a gain in comprehension as compared with the control condition. Most of Louthan's results agree with those of a similar study by Bradley (1970). Bradley gave multiple-choice comprehension questions on passages presented in their original form or four cloze versions. The passages and accompanying comprehension questions were chosen from reading tests listed in Buros (1965). In a further condition test subjects were to answer the questions without reading the passages. The results "showed that Ss were able to answer the multiple-choice items without the aid of the accompanying reading passage at a level significantly greater than chance" (Bradley 1970: 91). Not surprisingly, the scores were significantly higher for all the other conditions. However, the comprehension scores on passages with deletion of nouns or adjectives were significantly lower than those on passages presented in their original form. No significant difference was found between the latter and scores on passages with deletion of main verbs and function words.

1.6 Plan of the investigation

Although the studies mentioned in the preceding survey give valuable information on reactions to linguistic deviance, they do not by any means exhaust the research programme outlined in Section 1.4. Most of the work has dealt with reactions to different types of errors, whereas very little has been done to clarify the importance of factors such as receiver characteristics, type of language situation, and sender role. The present investigation does not examine all the aspects of error gravity which have been neglected previously. Rather, an attempt has been made to investigate, as fully and as consistently as possible, a few of the central problems. This work could hopefully serve as a starting-point in further investigations of error gravity.

The first problem taken up deals with the question of methodology in studies of error gravity (Chapter 2). This is followed by an investigation of the importance of overt errors in native speakers' judgements of the quality of written English (Chapter 3). A following chapter investigates reactions to some types of lexical and grammatical errors (Chapter 4). The remaining problems examined are foreign accent and speech distortion (Chapter 5), the relationship between different types of phonological errors (Chapter 6), and reactions of native vs non-native judges (Chapter 7). A concluding chapter summarizes the results of the investigation, considers possible applications, and gives suggestions for further research (Chapter 8).

The errors represented will be such as are frequent in the English produced by Swedish learners, but at least some of the results should be applicable to other groups of learners. Perhaps the most important limitation of the investigation is that some of the experiments use isolated words or sentences without a real communicative context.[18] This is a necessary limitation of the experimental technique (cf Section 2.1). At a later stage, it will be necessary to find ways of checking the results in more realistic language situations.

1.7 Comments on the experiments

The report contains an account of eight experiments. Each experiment will be reported in detail in the following chapters, but some general comments may be called for. The participants in most of the experiments have been university students studying non-language subjects. University students were chosen for reasons of availability; students of non-language subjects were selected as they are more representative of the type of receivers a foreigner will come in contact with and also because there is some evidence that untrained judges give more consistent responses than trained subjects (cf Sections 1.5.4 and 1.5.5). Most of the material was collected during two visits to the University of Lancaster, England, in 1975-76.[19]

NOTES

1 Sections 1.1-4 are based mainly on the earlier presentations in Johansson (1975a, 1975b).

2 The figure has been adapted from Johansson (1975a: 17), where it is explained in greater detail.

3 The term "covert errors" is here used somewhat differently from Corder (1973: 272f).

4 A distinction of this kind is made in Burt & Kiparsky (1972: 6f), who distinguish between global and local errors. For a survey of linguistic measures for error gravity, see James (1974). Note also the discussions of degrees of grammaticalness in Chomsky (1965: 148ff) and Steube (1968), and the linguistic measures of dialect distance in Bailey (1971).

5 It might be argued that the communicative effect of errors would be reflected by purely linguistic measures. However, there is no necessary correspondence between linguistic measures and communicative efficiency. Firstly, linguistic descriptions often make no claims about psychological reality and hence do not account for how sentences are processed. Secondly, purely linguistic measures overlook such features as the attitude of the language-user. Note the interesting example discussed by Wolff (1959), where intelligibility is shown to be dependent upon the attitude of the language-user as well as upon purely linguistic features. Cf also Hymes (1972: 288), "the degree of linguistic similarity and distance cannot predict mutual intelligibility, let alone use". Note finally Corder (1975: 207), "The problem of the relationship between the degree of deviance of an error as determined by some sort of linguistic measure and its comprehensibility or intolerability to native-speaking judges is still far from understood."

6 Criteria such as "intelligibility" or "communicative efficiency" have, however, sometimes been rejected, due to the problems of establishing such standards. See e g Lado (1961: 39), Burgschmidt & Götz (1974: 140).

7 The tables have been explained in greater detail in Johansson (1975a: 22ff).

8 It should be pointed out that other foreign speakers should also be included among possible receivers.

9 The deviance may not just be tolerated but may even have positive effects (cf Diller 1971: 99, Levelt 1975: 16). Cf also the high rating of certain foreign accents in the study by Giles (1970). Note further the example taken up in Shriner (1971: 1144) of "the psychiatrist who deliberately learns to speak a Viennese dialect to function more effectively as a psychotherapist". The attitude taken up in the present investigation is that it may very well be advantageous under many (or even most) circumstances to be identified as a foreigner. This does not mean, however, that one should not attempt to remove those deviations which obstruct communication.

10 There are, no doubt, other investigations based on judgement techniques than those taken up below. Palmer (1973) and Ryan (1973) are interesting from a methodological point of view, though no detailed results are reported. Brennan *et al* (1975) report a series of experiments where subjects judged foreign accent by magnitude estimation and also by squeezing a hand dynamometer. There was significant agreement among subjects regarding the speech samples with each scaling method, and interscale agreeement was good.

11 Hence, "language teachers are apt to be the poorest judges of their students' ability to communicate with strangers" (Brodkey 1972: 203).

12 The relationship between subjective and objective measures is further discussed in Chapter 2.

13 Note, however, that a study by Rose (1973) showed high agreement between linguists and non-linguists.

14 For a discussion of the problems of using trained subjects in linguistics and psychology, see Levelt (1974: 18ff).

15 Note in this context the study by Healy & Miller (1971), who investigated the relative contribution of nouns and verbs to sentence acceptability and comprehensibility in rating tasks and a sentence completion task. It was found that "the main verb is more essential to the grammatical integrity or acceptability of a sentence than is the subject noun but that the verb is not necessarily more essential to the meaningfulness or comprehensibility of the sentence" (Healy & Miller 1971: 95). The possible differences between measures of acceptability and comprehensibility need further investigation.

16 For some other experiments with transformed text, see Kolers (1968, 1969).

17 Some information on strategies of interpreting ungrammatical sentences can also be obtained from the results of a paraphrase task in Downey & Hakes (1968).

18 That context is an important factor in comprehension is supported by everyday experience as well as by experiments. Cf e g Miller *et al* (1951), Bruce (1956), Pollack & Pickett (1964).

19 It should also be added that none of the native speakers of English used as test subjects knew Swedish or had visited Sweden or associated with Swedes in England.

2 Subjective and Objective Measures of Error Gravity

2.1 Methods of studying error gravity

A possible approach to the study of error gravity is to collect samples of the speech or writing of language learners, submit them to groups of native speakers, and study what qualities, positive as well as negative, correlate best with native speakers' reactions. This is an approach which has been used in analyzing essays produced by native speakers (Page & Paulus 1968, Hersvall et al 1974). A problem with using this type of investigation in studies of error gravity is that samples of learner language normally contain a mixture of error types and often only a limited number of examples of each error type. This makes it difficult to establish a correlation between specific error types and native speakers' reactions. A different approach has therefore been used in most of the experiments reported in this investigation. Rather than using natural learner language we have constructed material containing specific error types. Nevertheless, in producing the material we have been guided by observations of natural learner behaviour, more specifically by observations of the errors produced by Swedish learners of English.

A further methodological problem concerns the form and nature of the native speakers' reactions. Here we can distinguish between two fundamentally different types of investigation, i e the subjective and the objective method. This distinction corresponds to that between judgement tests and operation tests in Quirk & Svartvik (1966); cf **Section** 1.5.5. In the subjective method informants are asked to give judgements about linguistic deviance; in the objective method they are asked to perform various tasks, e g repeat erroneous sentences or read texts with different types of errors. In the former situation informants are conscious of grading errors, whereas the measure of error gravity is arrived at indirectly by studying informant behaviour in the latter case.

On the face of it, the subjective method seems objectionable, as it might reveal more about informants' prejudices than about the communicative effect of errors. What is judged to be a more serious error might not cause a more serious problem of communication. Nevertheless, we have previously found a surprising agreement between the results of judgement tests and performance tasks involving the transmission of information (Johansson 1975a: 34ff). These findings will be briefly summarized here, as they have been used as a starting-point for the experiments reported later.

2.2 Subjective and objective measures of error gravity: previous findings

In the study just referred to an attempt was made to establish the relationship between subjective and objective measures of error gravity. Three error types were selected:[1]

A Concord errors, e g

John says that the visitors has probably left.
[John says that the visitors have probably left.]

B Errors in verb complementation, e g

My doctor suggests me to take a holiday.
[My doctor suggests that I should take a holiday.]

C Word-order errors, e g

Not a single mistake they have ever made.
[Not a single mistake have they ever made.]

The errors included were such as might occur among Swedish learners of English, but the two first-mentioned categories are probably representative of a wide variety of English learners.[2]

The three error types were studied in a series of experiments. A group of twenty students at the University of Lancaster, England, took part in two test sessions each:

Session I: a perception test (the Perception Test) and a judgement test (Judgement Test I)

Session II: a reading test (the Reading Test) and a judgement test (Judgement Test II)

Test subjects were, with one exception, first-year students of biology and were 18-20 years old. Half of them were male, half of them female. The majority were from the North of England and had had little contact with foreign speakers of English. The Perception Test was also administered to 58 school children in Lancaster and Judgement Test I to 20 teachers of English in Lancaster secondary schools.

As the experiments have been reported in detail elsewhere, the present survey will be very brief. In the Perception Test informants listened to a series of sentences containing one error from the types mentioned above. Each sentence was followed by a random sequence of three numbers. Examples:

John says that the visitors has probably left. 538
They prevented him to receive the promised payment. 816
The little boy sees often exciting adventure films. 297

Test subjects were asked to write down each sentence in corrected form followed by the number sequence. The amount of change (apart from mere corrections) was to be taken as a measure of the communicative effect of the error.

The introduction of the number sequence should perhaps be justified. The original idea was to ask subjects simply to write down test sentences in corrected form. However, this task seemed too easy. More importantly, it seemed artificial, since listeners, in a natural language situation, do not normally concentrate on correcting errors (and one error at a time at that). At the same time as they are listening, they may be planning what to say in reply or may be following another conversation or be involved simultaneously in non-verbal activities. The number sequence was introduced in order to represent in some way these other simultaneous activities.

The group of university students had few difficulties in performing the task assigned. The number of students introducing changes apart from corrections (e g tense or number changes, omissions, substitutions of different words) was low. Nevertheless, the order between the error types was the same as that found in all the experiments to be reported later. The mean number of subjects introducing changes of the kind referred to was:

4.75 for sentences containing verb complementation errors
4.38 for sentences containing concord errors
1.88 for sentences containing word-order errors

The higher figure indicates greater irritation due to the error and could be taken as a measure of error gravity.

When the Perception Test was administered to the group of school children (aged 12-13), the amount of change apart from mere corrections was high. The number sequence was, however, very rarely missed. The results show a consistent relationship between the three error types, i e the same as that found among the university students.

After the Perception Test the group of university students was given a written judgement test (Judgement Test I), where they were asked to grade the acceptability of the sentences included in the Perception Test. Judgement Test I consisted of two sections, a ranking test where groups of three sentences were to be ranked and a rating test where the material was to be graded according to a five-point scale. The agreement between the ranking test and the rating test was good. Moreover, there was a close correspondence between the student group and the group of secondary school teachers who were tested on the material of Judgement Test I. The acceptability values were compared with the results of the Perception Test. It was found that a greater number of changes apart from corrections in a test sentence in the latter test corresponded to a lower acceptability value.

The Reading Test administered during the second test session to the group of university students consisted of a series of four texts of about 350 words each. The texts were similar in style and subject-matter. One of the texts was left unchanged (Text I). The other three were manipulated and different kinds of errors were introduced:

Text II: 10 verb complementation errors
Text III: 10 word-order errors
Text IV: 10 concord errors

An attempt was made to include errors similar to those represented in the Perception Test and Judgement Test I. Finally, questions on content were prepared for each text.

The Reading Test was administered individually to each participant at the start of the second test session. Test subjects were told that they would be asked to read a series of short texts and that they would have to answer questions on the texts afterwards. They were also told that a record would be kept of their reading speed.[3] All participants read Text I first, but the order of the other texts was varied systematically. The Reading Test was also administered to a control group of 20 university students, who read correct versions of all the texts. The order of the texts was the same as for the experimental group.

The answers to the questions on the texts were not scored, as the questions were mainly included to divert the attention of test subjects from the main object of the Reading Test, i e the measurement of reading speed. The reading scores are given in Table 2:1. Both the experimental group and the control group show an increase in reading time in Texts II-IV, but the figures for the control group are consistently lower. In the table the increase in the two groups has been related to their scores for Text I. It appears then that the increase is greater in the experimental group. The increase in the control group should reasonably be attributed to the inherent difficulty of the texts. If this is so, the additional increase in the experimental group (see Table 2:1) could only be attributed to the presence of the errors. The amount of additional increase could be taken as a measure of the communicative effect of the errors. Interestingly enough, this gives us the same ordering between the error types as was found in the previous experiments.

Table 2:1 The Reading Test: the mean reading time for the experimental group and the control group (within parentheses). Test subjects: 20 university students in each group.

	Text I: no errors	Text II; errors in verb complementation	Text III: word-order errors	Text IV: concord errors
Mean reading time in seconds	82.50 (74.95)	97.40 (79.10)	88.35 (76.05)	94.50 (78.05)
Increase in seconds with respect to Text I	-	14.90 (4.15)	5.85 (1.10)	12.00 (3.10)
Per cent increase with respect to Text I	-	18.00 (5.50)	7.09 (1.40)	14.50 (4.10)
Additional increase (in per cent) in the experimental group	-	12.50	5.69	10.40

After the Reading Test the participants were given a print-out of Texts II-IV with the portions containing errors underlined. They were asked to correct and grade the acceptability of each underlined portion with reference to a five-point scale (Judgement Test II). The mean acceptability ratings assigned to the three error types were (a higher figure indicates higher acceptability):

2.08 for errors in verb complementation
2.32 for concord errors
3.29 for word-order errors

The relationship between these figures and the results reported earlier is obvious. The error type which caused a greater number of listeners to introduce changes (apart from corrections) in the Perception Test and caused a greater increase in reading time in the Reading Test has received a lower acceptability measure in both Judgement Tests I and II.

2.3 Subjective and objective measures of error gravity: a further experiment

The correspondence between the subjective measures of the judgement tests and the objective measures of the other experiments reported is remarkable. A further experiment has therefore been conducted in order to establish if the correspondence would reappear under different circumstances. This will be referred to as Experiment I. Experiment I consisted of a perception test of the same kind as that described in Section 2.2 and a following judgement test.

2.3.1 Experiment I: material and method

Whereas the previous experiments were designed to rank different types of grammatical errors, Experiment I was aimed at ranking grammatical vs phonological errors. The idea was to compare reactions to grammatically incorrect sentences recorded by native speakers of English with reactions to grammatically correct renderings of the same sentences recorded by Swedish students of English. The former would presumably contain only grammatical errors, the latter only phonological errors.

12 grammatically incorrect sentences were recorded by two native speakers of English (speakers of Received Pronunciation). Grammatically correct renderings of the same sentences were recorded by two Swedish students of English (with typical pronunciation errors). Two test versions (A and B) were constructed, each containing 6 sentences recorded by the Swedes (3 from each speaker) and 6 sentences recorded by the natives (3 from each speaker). For the purposes of comparison, four grammatically correct sentences recorded by a third native English speaker were inserted in each test version. These sentences therefore contained neither grammatical nor phonological errors. Also for the purposes of comparison, a third test version (C) was constructed. This was identical to A except that the grammatically incorrect sentences recorded by the natives were exchanged for grammatically correct renderings by the same speakers. The whole of version C therefore contained only grammatically correct sentences. The details of the test design are set forth in the Appendix.

The material of versions A, B, and C was adapted to form a perception test of the same kind as that described in Section 2.2. A random sequence of five numbers was inserted after each sentence, and each item was separated by a pause of 15 seconds. Some items which were not scored were added at the beginning and end of each test version. Three groups of students at the University of Lancaster took part in the perception test (version A: 12 students, version B: 12 students, version C: 10 students). The participants were 18-24 years old. The majority were first-year students enrolled in non-language subjects. Regional dialect was not controlled; there were participants from most parts of England, about half from the North and half from the South.

The perception test was administered separately to each group in a language laboratory. The following instructions were given (versions A and B):

You will hear a series of sentences pronounced by foreign speakers of English. Many of them may sound strange to you, because of the grammatical constructions used, the choice of words, or the speaker's pronunciation. Your task is to repeat the sentences as you would have said them yourself. Each sentence is followed by a number sequence. This should also be repeated. Examples:

You hear: The informations we have received are rather depressing. 35261
You say: The information we have received is rather depressing. 35261

You hear: Dhis is a pretty picture. 41893
You say: This is a pretty picture. 41893

You hear: Sometimes are the trees green in early April. 79362
You say: The trees are sometimes green in early April, 79362

Do not be discouraged if you do not remember all the numbers. Repeat as many as you can.

Note that no indication was given that some of the speakers were natives. The instructions for version C were different in this respect:

You will hear a series of sentences pronounced by native or foreign speakers of English. Each sentence is followed by a number sequence. Your task is to repeat each sentence followed by the number sequence. Examples:

You hear: The information we have received is rather depressing. 35261
You say: The information we have received is rather depressing. 35261

You hear: Dhis is a pretty picture. 41893
You say: This is a pretty picture. 41893

Do not be discouraged if you do not remember all the numbers. Repeat as many as you can.

The difference in the instructions in version C was a necessary consequence of the difference in the material.

After the perception test the participants were given a judgement task consisting of the same material (except that the number sequences were eliminated and the pauses between the items were shorter, approximately 5 seconds). The following instructions were given:

You will hear the same sentences once more. Your task is now to rate the degree of foreignness of the sentences using a five-point scale:

native-like + __ __ __ __ __ - very foreign

Listen carefully now and rate each item by putting a mark on the scale provided.

Each participant received an answer sheet containing the numbers of the test items, followed by scales of the type indicated above. The instructions were exactly the same for the three listener groups.

2.3.2 Experiment I: results

The results have been summarized in detail in Table 2:2. As the number of participants in each group was quite low, the results have to be interpreted with great caution. The perception score indicates the number of participants who introduced changes (apart from corrections) affecting the meaning of sentences. The number sequences after the sentences were frequently incorrectly rendered, but this has not been taken into account in scoring the test. By comparing the scores from versions A and B we can establish the mutual relationships of the phonological and grammatical errors represented.

The perception scores were often very low and frequently did not show any contrast between grammatically and phonologically deviant sentences. Nevertheless, in all the cases where an appreciable contrast did appear (items 1, 3, 7, 8, 10) the phonologically deviant sentence showed the highest score. All in all, there were more than twice as many informants who introduced changes (apart from corrections) in the sentences containing phonological errors than in those containing grammatical errors. Note also that both types of test items differed from the grammatically correct sentences recorded by the native English speakers. The latter received consistently low scores (1 or 0).

Table 2:2 Experiment I: results. The perception score states the number of listeners who introduced changes (apart from corrections); the judgement score gives the mean rating on a five-point scale (+5...1-). E1, E2, E3 indicate the native English speakers, S1 and S2 the Swedish speakers. Test subjects: 34 university students (Version A: 12, Version B: 12, Version C: 10).

	Test item	Version A			Version B			Version C		
		Speaker	Perc score	Judgm score	Speaker	Perc score	Judgm score	Speaker	Perc score	Judgm score
1	Detective stories she always reads before falling asleep.	E1	0	3.17						
	She always reads detective stories before falling asleep.				S2	4	1.42	E1	0	4.90
2	The children prevent Mary to do her work.				E1	0	3.00			
	The children prevent Mary from doing her work.	S1	1	2.17				S1	0	1.80
3	Tom and Paul plans to buy a new motor-boat.				E1	1	3.83			
	Tom and Paul plan to buy a new motor-boat.	S2	6	1.83				S2	4	1.50
4	John says that the visitors probably have left.	E2	0	3.75						
	John says that the visitors have probably left.				S1	1	1.83	E2	0	3.80
5	My doctor says that I should take a holiday.	E3	1	4.75	E3	0	4.50	E3	1	4.40
6	Your new employer wants that you should resign immediately.	E2	3	2.50						
	Your new employer wants you to resign immediately.				S2	2	2.92	E2	1	4.50
7	Never I could have thought that Dick was wrong.				E1	1	2.50			
	Never could I have thought that Dick was wrong.	S1	12	1.42				S1	10	1.10
8	The new chairs we bought seems very comfortable.	E1	6	3.42						
	The new chairs we bought seem very comfortable.				S1	9	2.25	E1	0	5.00
9	Peter helped the blind man across the street.	E3	0	5.00	E3	0	4.42	E3	1	4.00
10	The young student want to start studying Arabic.				E2	4	3.50			
	The young student wants to start studying Arabic.	S1	7	2.17				S1	5	1.30
11	The musicians finish to practise at two o'clock today.				E1	8	4.67			
	The musicians finish practising at two o'clock today.	S2	9	2.75				S2	7	1.60
12	The actor has never received the promised award.	E3	0	5.00	E3	0	4.75	E3	0	4.70
13	The little girl play the violin very well.	E2	2	2.75						
	The little girl plays the violin very well.				S2	2	2.67	E2	0	4.00
14	The doctor suggested Mr Jones to leave at once.	E1	1	3.00						
	The doctor suggested that Mr Jones should leave at once.				S1	3	1.58	E1	0	4.90
15	The little boy sees often exciting adventure films.				E2	0	2.42			
	The little boy often sees exciting adventure films.	S2	0	2.00				S2	0	1.60
16	Professor Higgins promised to give a lecture on phonetics.	E3	0	5.00	E3	0	4.83	E3	0	4.80

It seems reasonable to conclude from the perception test (1) that sentences containing neither grammatical nor phonological errors are more easily perceived than grammatically or phonologically deviant sentences, and (2) that certain kinds of phonological deviance cause greater perception problems than the grammatical errors represented. The results from the judgement test agree with these findings, except that the two contrasts appear much more clearly.[4] Grammatically correct sentences recorded by native English speakers received consistently higher ratings than the grammatically incorrect versions of the same sentences recorded by the same speakers (cf the scores for corresponding items in versions A and C). Note also the consistently high ratings assigned by the three listener groups to test items recorded by E3 (items 5, 9, 12, 16). Sentences containing grammatical or phonological errors normally received considerably lower ratings. There is one striking exception, viz item 11 in version B. The unexpectedly high rating in this case is probably due to the fact that this sentence was perceived by many listeners as: <u>The musicians finished a/their practice at two o'clock today</u>. Phonologically deviant sentences regularly received lower ratings than grammatically incorrect versions of the same sentences (cf the scores for corresponding items in versions A and B). However, the difference was negligible in one item (13), and another item (6) showed the opposite relationship. The probable explanation is that the phonological deviance was comparatively slight in these cases (cf the Appendix); note that items 6 and 13 received the highest ratings among the sentences recorded by the Swedish speakers in version B.

The very sharp difference between the ratings of phonologically and grammatically deviant sentences deserves some comment. It might partially reflect an uncertainty among the listeners as to the judgement task. Some of the listeners reported after the test that they did not know whether they were only supposed to rate the pronunciation of the sentences or whether they were also required to take grammatical structure into account. This had purposely not been specified in the instructions for the test. The comparatively high rating of sentences containg grammatical errors might be due to the fact that some listeners ignored grammatical sturcture in making their judgements. A more probable explanation is, however, that the listeners felt that the pronunciation errors caused a greater potential danger for understanding than did the grammatical errors represented. A study of response patterns reveals that the degree of misunderstanding was normally greater in cases of phonological deviance. Some typical examples (substitutions are listed immediately below relevant parts of the test items; omissions are indicated by dashes):

```
8   The new chairs we bought seem very comfortable. (S1)
            shares           seemed    secure
                                       profitable
                             seem to be doing well

8   The new chairs we bought seems very comfortable. (E1)
            chair            seemed -

10  The young student wants to start studying Arabic. (S1)
        giant                                   -
        German

10  The young student want to start studying Arabic. (E2)
        new   students wanted

13  The musicians finish practising at two o'clock today. (S2)
        museums   stopped              one           -
        sessions                       three
                                       four
                                        -

13  The musicians finish to practise at two o'clock today. (E1)
                  finished their practice  three
                  finished a practice      four
                  finished practising      seven
                                             -
                                           early today
```

The majority of the changes in the grammatically deviant sentences were alterations of tense, number, or the like, whereas changes in the phonologically deviant sentences frequently introduced completely unrelated lexical material.

Finally, let us briefly consider the correspondence between the subjective measures of the judgement test and the objective measures of the perception test. As appears from the above discussion, the general direction of the results is the same in the two testing situations. However, the judgement test seems to have greater discriminatory power. The perception test frequently did not discriminate between test items of different kinds. Where it did discriminate, the results agreed with the judgement test. A weakness of the judgement test showed up in one case (test item 11 in version B; cf above). Here a grammatically deviant sentence received a very high rating, although it was frequently incorrectly perceived in the perception test.

2.3.3 Experiment I: conclusions

The results of Experiment I show that phonological errors may be more serious from the point of view of communication than are the grammatical errors represented. A probable explanation is that the possibilities of grammatical deviance are more limited than those of phonological deviance. A grammatically deviant sentence is therefore more easily rectifiable. Nevertheless, very few and very superficial cases of grammatical deviance were represented in Experiment I. The results certainly cannot be generalized to all types of grammatical and phonological errors. At most, they could be used to stress the importance of an acceptable pronunciation.

Experiment I has also shown once more the correspondence between subjective and objective testing techniques. This correspondence is remarkable and "could perhaps be taken as an indication that, through frequent experience in communication, the language user has developed an intuitive sense of communicative efficiency" (Johansson 1975a: 50). Although the result may seem unexpected, it agrees with observations of informant behaviour in other situations;[5] note e g the results of studies reported in Sections 1.5.3 and 1.5.5 which demonstrate the agreement between subjective and objective techniques in dialect intelligibility testing and acceptability testing. Further support can be found in the studies by Schwartz et al (1970) and Wang (1970a, 1970b), which show the validity of judgements of comprehensibility.

The agreement between subjective and objective techniques means that the problem of establishing error gravity is reduced to manageable proportions, as the study could be based mainly on judgement tests. Such tests are easy to construct, administer and score, whereas the objective experiments require elaborate preparation, are time-consuming and difficult to evaluate. There are certain problems with the judgement technique (cf Section 2.3.2, the end) which show that it is important to have a check on comprehension for material to be judged.[6] Nevertheless, on the basis of the results of Experiment I and the previous experiments reported the rest of this investigation will use mainly the judgement technique.

Finally, we must consider how the informants' reactions should be interpreted in terms of the concepts of comprehensibility and degree of irritation introduced in Section 1.3. The original idea was to establish comprehensibility by straightforward comprehension tests and degree of irritation by some sort of psychological measure. To apply this scheme in practice proved, however, to be difficult. On the one hand, it became apparent that ordinary comprehension tests would not discriminate between many error types; note that most of the error types represented in this chapter would not normally be considered to affect comprehensibility. On the other hand, it seemed problematic to obtain a direct measure of irritation and differentiate between the error types in this way. The solution chosen here was to base the investigation mainly on informants' judgements of deviance. As shown in this chapter, such judgements reflect the communicative effect of errors, though they cannot be related directly either to the concept of comprehensibility or degree of irritation. In talking about the communicative effect of errors we shall, however, sometimes use the term degree of irritation, which is then taken in a somewhat more general sense than that originally intended in Section 1.3.

NOTES

1 A corrected version is given within brackets after each example.

2 The "word-order errors" were typical of the English produced by Swedish learners. Some of them exemplified less usual rather than incorrect orders. This should be kept in mind in interpreting the results of the experiments.

3 Test subjects were told to read each text only once from beginning to end, and their reading time was recorded from eye movements.

4 The judgement scores indicate the mean ratings assigned by test subjects. As in the experiments to be reported later, we have given the mean rather than the median in presenting the results of the ratings on the five-point scale. A calculation of both types of scores for a selection of test items revealed very small differences between the mean and the median.

5 Needless to say, informant judgements have often been regarded with great caution. What we are claiming here is, however, not that there will necessarily be a correspondence between an individual's judgement and some kind of objective measure but rather that the collective behaviour of a group of subjects may be approximately the same in studies using subjective and objective techniques.

6 Preferably, informants should be asked both to interpret the material and to give a judgement of deviance. In this way we do not need to speculate about the basis of the informants' judgements. We can then also collect information on the informants' own usage and on strategies of interpretation.

APPENDIX. EXPERIMENT I: MATERIAL

There were three versions of Experiment I, each containing 16 sentences (here listed in the order in which they appeared):

		Version		
		A	B	C
1	Detective stories she always reads before falling asleep.	E1		
	She always reads detective stories before falling asleep.		S2	E1
2	The children prevent Mary to do her work.		E1	
	The children prevent Mary from doing her work.	S1		S1
3	Tom and Paul plans to buy a new motor-boat.		E1	
	Tom and Paul plan to buy a new motor-boat.	S2		S2
4	John says that the visitors probably have left.	E2		
	John says that the visitors have probably left.		S1	E2
5	My doctor says that I should take a holiday.	E3	E3	E3
6	Your new employer wants that you should resign immediately.	E2		
	Your new employer wants you to resign immediately.		S2	E2
7	Never I could have thought that Dick was wrong.		E1	
	Never could I have thought that Dick was wrong.	S1		S1
8	The new chairs we bought seems very comfortable.	E1		
	The new chairs we bought seem very comfortable.		S1	E1
9	Peter helped the blind man across the street.	E3	E3	E3
10	The young student want to start studying Arabic.		E2	
	The young student wants to start studying Arabic.	S1		S1
11	The musicians finish to practise at two o'clock today.		E1	
	The musicians finish practising at two o'clock today.	S2		S2
12	The actor has never received the promised award.	E3	E3	E3
13	The little girl play the violin very well.	E2		
	The little girl plays the violin very well.		S2	E2
14	The doctor suggested Mr Jones to leave at once.	E1		
	The doctor suggested that Mr Jones should leave at once.		S1	E1
15	The little boy sees often exciting adventure films.		E2	
	The little boy often sees exciting adventure films.	S2		S2
16	Professor Higgins promised to give a lecture on phonetics.	E3	E3	E3

E1, E2, E3 indicate the native English speakers, S1 and S2 the Swedish speakers. The grammatical errors represented were errors in word-order, concord, and verb complementation, i e the same as those represented in the tests reported in Section 2.2. The main pronunciation errors in the recordings by the Swedish speakers were:

S1:

2 The children ['ʃildrən] prevent Mary from doing ['dəuiŋ] her work.

4 John says that the visitors ['wizitəz] have probably left [læft].

7 Never could I have thought [tɔ:t] that Dick was wrong. (also hesitation pause before <u>thought</u>)

8 The new chairs [ʃɛəz] we bought seem very comfortable ['kɔmfɔtəbl].

10 The young [dʒʌŋ] student wants to start studying Arabic [ə'ræbik].

14 The doctor suggested [sə'jestid] that Mr Jones [jəunz] should leave at once.

S2:

1 She always reads detective stories before falling asleep. (staccato rhythm, monotonous intonation, hesitation pauses)

3 Tom and Paul plan to buy a new motor-boat. (staccato rhythm, monotonous intonation)

6 Your new employer wants you to resign [ri'sain] immediately. (staccato rhythm and monotonous intonation but spoken very fluently)

11 The musicians [mju'siʃəns] finish practising at two o'clock today. (staccato rhythm, monotonous intonation)

13 The little girl plays the violin very well. (staccato rhythm, monotonous intonation)

15 The little boy often sees [si:s] exciting adventure ['ædventʃə] films. (staccato rhythm, monotonous intonation)

Pronunciation errors of these types are typical of a Swedish accent in English. All the sentences recorded by S1 were spoken with acceptable stress and intonation. The amount of deviance varied considerably in the recordings by S2.

3 Overt vs Covert Errors

3.1 Background

This investigation is concerned mainly with establishing the mutual relationships of different types of overt errors. However, there is also a need to examine the importance of overt errors as opposed to such weaknesses as poverty of expression (with no cases of overt deviance; cf the quotation from Weinreich in Section 1.2) or poverty of content. Such errors of omission, or covert errors, are probably more serious than errors of commission, or overt errors, as shown by Landén & Trankell (1975). As reported in Section 1.5.2, Landén & Trankell found that the listener's impression of a speaker is based on the content of what is said rather than on the occurrence of overt errors. To further investigate this finding, an experiment was performed which is partially analogous to that of Landén & Trankell.

3.2 Experiment II

3.2.1 Material and method

21 short papers written by Swedish students of English were selected. The papers were of approximately the same length (100-150 words) and dealt with the same subject ("A Great Achievement"). They were selected so as to represent a variety of possible treatments, both from the point of view of form and content. 16 of the papers were typed out in their original as well as in a corrected form,[2] the remaining 5 were only reproduced in their original form. The Appendix contains a few examples of papers in their correct and incorrect versions.

Two sets of test booklets (I and II) were prepared each containing 21 papers. I included 8 correct and 8 incorrect papers and II the opposite versions of the same papers. Common to I and II were the 5 papers which only appeared in their original form. The order between the 21 papers in each booklet was random and determined by shuffling.

The tests were administered to 44 students at the University of Lancaster. The subjects, who were paid to take part in the experiment, were all from the United Kingdom and were, with one exception, 18-22 years old. Most of them were first-year students enrolled in non-language subjects. Each was given a test booklet with one of the following sets of instructions:

A: The following papers were produced by foreign students of English. All of the papers are of approximately the same length and deal with the same topic ("A Great Achievement"). Your task is to grade the papers on a five-point scale (try to ignore whether you agree with the opinions expressed or not):

very good	+ __ __ __ __ __ -	very bad

In judging the papers you may find it helpful to start by dividing them roughly into three groups ("good", "bad", "medium"). Then try to give each paper a grade using the five-point scale.

Do not hesitate to use the extreme points of the scale! If you wish, you may also add comments on the papers in the space provided.

B: The following short papers were produced by foreign students of English. All the papers are of approximately the same length and deal with the same subject ("A Great Achievement"). Your task is to rate each paper on a five-point scale according to <u>how successfully the writer has handled the topic</u> (try to ignore whether you agree with the opinions expressed or not):

The treatment of the topic is very successful and effective	+ __ __ __ __ __ -	The treatment of the topic is very poor and ineffective

> In judging the papers you may find it helpful to start by dividing them roughly into three groups ("good", "bad", "medium"). Then try to give each paper a grade using the five-point scale.
>
> Do not hesitate to use the extreme points of the scale! If you wish, you may also add comments on the papers in the space provided.

The two test forms and the two sets of instructions were alternated among the participants such that every fourth received a different combination. There were therefore four approximately equal groups of test subjects:[3]

G1: test form I, instructions A (N: 12)
G2: test form I, instructions B (N: 10)
G3: test form II, instructions A (N: 11)
G4: test form II, instructions B (N: 11)

The test subjects, who were instructed to use as much time as they needed, spent between 40 and 75 minutes in performing the task.

3.2.2 Experiment II: results

The mean ratings assigned by the test subjects are given in Table 3:1. The scores for the 5 items common to both test forms (2, 5, 7, 9, 17) were fairly close, though not identical. In the other cases the corrected version of a paper has regularly received a higher rating. This occurred without exceptions when the papers were judged according to instructions A and, with only one exception (10), when they were judged according to instructions B. The presence of overt errors has therefore had a clear effect on the judgement of a paper. The effect is, however, much more marked with instructions A than with instructions B. This is more clearly brought out in Tables 3:2 and 3:3, which give the mean ratings for original vs corrected versions with both types of instructions.

Table 3:1 Experiment II: mean ratings of texts in original (O) and corrected (C) versions. A higher figure indicates a higher rating on the five-point scale (+5...1-). Test subjects: 44 university students (G1: 12, G2: 10, G3: 11, G4: 11).

Paper	Test form I		Test form II	
	Instr A (G1)	Instr B (G2)	Instr A (G3)	Instr B (G4)
1	C: 3.55	C: 3.82	O: 2.33	O: 2.60
2	O: 1.91	O: 2.09	O: 2.08	O: 1.80
3	O: 2.82	O: 2.82	C: 4.08	C: 3.20
4	C: 3.55	C: 3.09	O: 2.25	O: 2.70
5	O: 3.27	O: 3.64	O: 3.58	O: 2.80
6	O: 1.55	O: 1.82	C: 2.92	C: 2.60
7	O: 4.09	O: 4.18	O: 4.50	O: 4.60
8	O: 2.73	O: 3.18	C: 4.17	C: 3.50
9	O: 2.82	O: 3.45	O: 3.58	O: 2.80
10	C: 3.91	C: 2.64	O: 2.42	O: 2.70
11	C: 3.64	C: 3.55	O: 2.17	O: 2.10
12	C: 3.64	C: 4.18	O: 2.25	O: 2.40
13	O: 2.18	O: 2.36	C: 4.08	C: 4.30
14	C: 4.27	C: 3.36	O: 3.00	O: 2.80
15	C: 4.09	C: 3.27	O: 2.92	O: 3.00
16	O: 2.82	O: 3.00	C: 4.08	C: 3.20
17	O: 4.18	O: 3.55	O: 3.50	O: 3.50
18	O: 2.09	O: 3.36	C: 4.08	C: 5.00
19	O: 2.09	O: 2.27	C: 3.42	C: 2.80
20	O: 1.55	O: 3.18	C: 2.92	C: 3.90
21	C: 4.18	C: 3.91	O: 2.33	O: 3.10

Table 3:2 Experiment II: mean ratings of original and corrected versions of papers judged according to instructions A.

Papers	Version: Corr	Version: Orig	
1, 4, 10, 11, 12, 14, 15, 21 (a)	G1: 3.85	G3: 2.23	M_a: 3.04
3, 6, 8, 13, 16, 18, 19, 20 (b)	G3: 3.72	G1: 2.46	M_b: 3.09
	M_{Corr}: 3.79	M_{Orig}: 2.34	

Table 3:3 Experiment II: mean ratings of original and corrected versions of papers judged according to instructions B.

Papers	Version: Corr	Version: Orig	
1, 4, 10, 11, 12, 14, 15, 21 (a)	G2: 3.47	G4: 2.68	M_a: 3.08
3, 6, 8, 13, 16, 18, 19, 20 (b)	G4: 3.56	G2: 2.75	M_b: 3.15
	M_{Corr}: 3.52	M_{Orig}: 2.72	

3.3 The effect of overt errors: discussion

Our experiment differs in several respects from that of Landén & Trankell (1975), above all in using written rather than spoken material and, more importantly, in the type of questions asked of test subjects. Whereas Landén & Trankell asked for the listener's impression of a speaker's personality, we asked for a rating of the quality of written material. Nevertheless, the technique is basically the same in examining reactions to material produced by foreigners in original and corrected form. It is therefore of interest to note that our experiment showed marked reactions to the presence of overt errors, whereas Landén & Trankell's did not.

The conflicting results of the two investigations may partially be due to the difference in material, as overt errors may be more readily accepted in speech than in writing, but another explanation seems more probable. Though overt errors may be disregarded in judging the personality of a speaker, this does not necessarily mean that they are disregarded in judging how well (cf instructions A) or how successfully (cf instructions B) the speaker communicates. The results of our experiment do not invalidate those of Landén & Trankell but rather show that they cannot be generalized and taken as evidence that overt errors are unimportant under all circumstances.

The difference between the ratings with instructions A and B further demonstrates the importance of the type of questions asked. As shown in the preceding section, the effect of the errors was much more pronounced with instructions A, where subjects were asked to judge the papers on a scale from "very good" to "very bad", than with instructions B, where they were asked to judge how successfully the writer handled the topic . This difference was expected. Though nothing was said about whether the judges should concentrate on form or content, instructions A draw more attention to aspects of form and instructions B emphasize content and more general features of presentation. Consequently, one would expect a clearer effect of the errors with instructions A.[4]

The difference in the rating of papers according to the two types of instructions shows up in judges' comments. The judges working with instructions A mostly commented on spelling, grammar and, less frequently, such features as range of vocabulary, sentence length, sentence linking, repetitiveness, etc. The comments made by judges working with instructions B were normally of a completely different kind. Examples (each group of comments is taken from the same judge):

Well written but could have developed the subject more. Did not really make his point well. - Good story. Makes you think about it until the end. - Well written but not really much to do with the subject. - Could have been a reasonable example but ended up more as a political propaganda story.

There are a number of grammatical errors, but the strength of the argument comes through well. - Short, to the point, with no wasted words.

Well structured argument. The achievement is supported by historical comparison. - Confuses achievement of space flight with potential achievement of international cooperation.

Quite clear. Very good treatment. - No, not a great achievement. - He seems confused on the concept of self-confidence.

Interesting way of looking at topic from point of view of the individual rather than the world in general. - This is interesting in that it looks at another side of 'great achievements'. It does not take up all the usual examples.

Ineffective, rather jumbled ideas. - Not really answered the title. - Ineffective. Leaves description of achievement until the last sentence. - Very poor, jumping from topic to topic.

Positive expression of opinion in simple English. - Confusing. If the issue is unbiased information, it is obviously ineffective because the passage is distinctly biased. - Good formulation of reason for argument, opinion and conclusion.

This writer tries to make the reader appreciate the wonders of space exploration, but simply lists well-known facts. - This writer tries to put too much information into too little space. - Very badly put together, no sequence or logical argument, merely a chain of facts. Nevertheless, an honest view. - This is badly written as the writer gets far too personally involved and drifts from the more preferable, objective style. - This writer would make a far better poet. Not very informative but the writer has treated the subject well.

Apart from making observations of this kind, judges working with instructions B sometimes also commented on the occurrence or non-occurrence of overt errors.

The most important result of Experiment II is that overt errors had a distinct effect on ratings even with instructions B, which emphasize success of communication rather formal aspects of the material. It would be of great interest to examine what other specific features correlate with judges' ratings as well as the relative importance of these features and the occurrence of overt errors, but this falls outside the scope of the present investigation.[5]

NOTES

1 The experiment reported in this chapter was carried out in collaboration with Moira Linnarud, Department of English, Lund University, Sweden.

2 In a few cases where the original contained few or no overt errors, a number of errors, in no case more than five, were inserted. These were of the same kind as those spontaneously produced in the other original versions.

3 Due to an error in administration, the number of participants in the four groups varies slightly.

4 It should, however, be added that the smaller effect of the errors with instructions B is partially due to the somewhat narrower dispersion of the mean ratings in this case. The mean and standard deviation for the 42 mean ratings were 3.15 and .72. The corresponding figures for instructions A were 3.13 and .86. The narrower dispersion in the former case is in its turn due to a greater heterogeneity of judgement among test subjects and a consequent evening out of extreme scores in the calculation of mean ratings.

5 A study of the lexical density and lexical variation (cf Linnarud 1975) of the material in Experiment II did not reveal any agreement with judges' ratings, i e papers with a higher lexical density and/or variation did not receive higher ratings than those with a lower lexical density and/or variation. This is probably because the papers were very short and, more importantly, because the topic did not necessarily call for the greater complexity and variety of expression reflected by lexical density and lexical variation, respectively. - Further studies should examine both "linguistic" and "informational" aspects of language use; cf Nas (1975).

APPENDIX. EXPERIMENT II: EXAMPLES OF MATERIAL

In the following examples the passages are given in their original version with corrections listed within parentheses.

1 Albert Schweitzer was a well known person. But when he died, his work, especially his hospital in Lambarene was very (very much) criticized, at least in some newspapers. The hospital equipments were (equipment was) ridiculously old-fashioned and the relatives of the patients lived together with their animals in the hospital yard and formed a big, dirty Negro village. But, nevertheless, Schweitzer succeeded to convey (in conveying) his ideas of humanity to these people, and it is as much (all the) more remarkable, as africans (Africans) nowadays are very suspicious against (of) the white man's ideas. During the civil war in Nigeria, those people, who (to whom) Schweitzer had taught Christian behaviour, were the only african (African) people that offered the Biafran refugees shelter and protection. So Schweitzers (Schweitzer's) intentions had not failed.

6 With the industrial age many great achievements have come. The perhaps (Perhaps the) most important one is the invention of electricity. It has meant much (a lot) in developing the industrial world. Electricity spares us a lot of hard work and inconvenience. It is used for machines in the factories. We use it in lighting up both the places we live and work in. In our homes we use electricity for a lot of things, for example refrigerators and vacuum-cleaners. The modern human being depend (depends) a lot on electricity. Nowadays one would not make (could not do) without it. The modern industrial world would fall to pieces if we did not get any more electricity. We would have to start from the beginning and build up a new civilization. The greatest disadvantage of water power is that of destroying our waters (rivers). On the other hand it does not pollute as other means (sources) of energy does (do).

8 Among all social reforms, welfare programmes and new conditions of living during the last twenty-five years, I think unmarried mothers have felt the altered attitudes most. As it nowadays is (is nowadays) stated by law, that all children, no matter whether they are born inside or outside (in or out of) marriage, should have the same rights, it is no longer nescessary (necessary) for young pregnant girls to legitimate their children by an unwanted marriage. A legal system of security has been formed to protect all members of the society (of society). Also the changed attitude among ordinary people has (The changed attitude among ordinary people has also) helped to make unmarried mothers a large (largely) accepted part of society. It is only twenty years ago, that (Only twenty years ago) they was (were) more or less looked upon as disgraceful and inferior creatures.

15 Spanish America is regarded as a sub-developed (an underdeveloped) country in spite of all its wealth and possibilities. They need money and the imperialistical (imperialist) countries are willing to invest money but at their own price. Cuba was one victim of the United States. The people suffered hard (greatly) and they were oppressed by the dictator Batista when Castro, a young lawyer, with the help of Russia, seized power in 1959. Thanks to this young man almost the whole nation have (has) learnt to read and write. They have food, work and they have something to fight for. From United States (the United States') point of view imperialism is the best (the best policy), but democracy, in the sub-developed countries to the extent that all people are equal, can not be achieved in another way than by revolution (democracy in the under-developed countries, to the extent that all people are equal, cannot be achieved in any other way than by revolution).

18 The boy stood looking on (at) the place where a house had once been. He had only been away for three hours but the tanks had been very thorough. The whole village was destroyed and most of it's (its) inhabitants was (were) dead. The boy felt a burning hatred and a desire for revenge. He wanted to kill; to put hatred into action. The German soldiers looked at him as if they wondered whether they should shot (shoot) him too. Twenty years later he stood at the same spot. He had just been on vacation in Germany. That journey had learned (taught) him to forget and forgive. He felt no longer (no longer felt) the want (desire) for vengeance. He started to live for the future and forget the past.

4 Types of Grammatical and Lexical Errors

4.1 Background

The relationship between grammatical and lexical errors was investigated by Engh (1971), who found that sentences containing grammatical errors caused fewer problems of interpretation than did those containing lexical errors; cf Section 1.5.1. This finding is by no means unexpected. It agrees well with the results from cloze test research, which has shown function words to be more predictable and contribute less to meaning than content words; cf Section 1.5.7. Nevertheless, it is possible that the relationship would vary depending upon the type of lexical or grammatical deviance. Experiments III and IV were undertaken to throw some light on this matter by contrasting certain types of lexical and grammatical errors, though no attempt is made at completeness.

4.2 Experiment III

4.2.1 Material and method

The material was based on two short passages translated from Swedish into English by Swedish university students. Model translations are found in the Appendix. Incorrect versions were constructed by inserting errors systematically into the model translations; see the Appendix. Each incorrect version contained five errors (grammatical or lexical). The errors were such as had been awarded 2 or 3 minus points (on a 3-point scale) by a committee grading the translations. Two test forms were prepared by combining a text containing lexical errors with one containing grammatical errors (I: Text 1C + Text 2G, II: Text 1E + Text 2B). The tests were administered to groups of native speakers of English who were given the following instructions:

The following papers have been produced by foreign students of English. Read the papers carefully and rewrite everything that seems incorrect (write in the space above the lines). Grade each paper on a five-point scale according to the use of English:

very good + _ _ _ _ _ - very bad

Put a mark on the scale provided for each paper. Try to use the whole scale, even though you may not think that the quality of the papers varies very much.

The test subjects were 43 students at the University of Lancaster, who had on a previous occasion taken part in the experiment described in the preceding chapter; cf Section 3.2.1. Different test forms were distributed to every other subject.[1] The number of participants was 22 for test form I, 21 for test form II.

4.2.2 Experiment III: results

The mean ratings for the texts are given in Table 4:1. The scores are consistently lower for Text 2 than for Text 1. As appears from the corrections, this is because subjects have objected to certain features of the model translation of this text. Nevertheless, for both texts the versions containing lexical errors have received lower ratings than those containing grammatical errors. A study of the corrections made by test subjects reveals that the lexical errors have often caused problems of interpretation, whereas this is not the case with the grammatical errors. However, the problems of interpretation have been fewer than might have been expected. Responses to the five lexical errors in Text 1 have been summarized in Table 4:2. As appears from the table, the number of correct interpretations was very high.[2] There were hardly any cases of misinterpretation; instead the problems of interpretation show up as failures to give a response. The same response pat-

Table 4:1 Experiment III: mean ratings of texts containing lexical or grammatical errors. A higher figure indicates a higher rating on the five-point scale (+5...1-). Test subjects: 22 university students for test form I (G1), 21 for test form II (G2).

	Error type		
	Lex	Gram	
Text 1	G1: 2.82	G2: 3.33	$M_{Text\ 1}$: 3.08
Text 2	G2: 2.14	G1: 2.55	$M_{Text\ 2}$: 2.35
	M_{Lex}: 2.48	M_{Gram}: 2.94	

Table 4:2 Responses to the lexical errors in Text 1 of Experiment III. Test subjects: 22 university students.

Error	Correct inter-pretation	Misinter-pretation	No response
likes for compares with	19	1	2
vertebra for backbone	4	0	18
rapebones for ribs	10	2	10
homage for headquarters	21	1	0
concurrents for rivals	14	2	6
Total	68	6	36

tern appeared with the five repetitions of the same lexical error in Text 2 (strings for shelves): correct interpretation 13, misinterpretation 0, no response 8. Though the lexical errors caused fewer problems than might have been expected, the problems were considerably greater than in the case of the grammatical errors. Both the corrections and the ratings of Experiment III therefore agree in assigning a higher degree of irritation to the lexical errors. This result is further supported by Experiment IV.

4.3 Experiment IV

4.3.1 Material and method

The material consisted of all the incorrect versions of Text 1 and 2 listed in the Appendix. The incorrect versions were constructed by inserting errors systematically into the model translations. Each incorrect version contained five errors. The errors were such as had been awarded 2 or 3 minus points (on a 3-point scale) by a committee grading the translations. An attempt was made to include a variety of error types, though the possibilities were limited due to the brevity of the texts and the decision to include only such errors as had actually been committed. Each text version was typed out on a separate sheet of paper and combined with the other versions of the same text into a test booklet. The order among the versions was random and determined by shuffling. One booklet for each text was given to 25 students at the University of Lancaster with the following instructions:[3]

The following papers have been translated into English by foreign students. Read the papers carefully and underline everything that seems incorrect. Grade each paper on a five-point scale according to the use of English:

very good + __ __ __ __ __ - very bad

Put a mark on the scale provided for each paper. Try to use the whole scale, even though you may not think that the quality of the papers varies very much.

The test subjects had all taken part in Experiment III previously and were given the new test at the end of the test session (after taking part in an intervening task, which will not be reported in this context).

4.3.2 Experiment IV: results

The results, which have been summarized in Table 4:3, agree with those of Experiment III. The versions containing lexical errors have received lower ratings than all the other versions. This is true of both Texts 1 and 2. 2B seems to be an exception, but this version should really be compared only with 2G, which also contains five repetitions of the same error. The reactions to 2B and 2G show that five repetitions of the same error are judged to be less serious than five occurrences of different errors. This is what would be expected and agrees with the grading of the errors (cf the Appendix).

The relationship between the lexical errors in 2D and 2F should be noted. 2F was judged more leniently, no doubt because the errors merely represent distortions of the correct word or phrase and would hardly cause any misunderstanding. In fact, the rating of 2F is hardly different from that of 2A, which contained miscellaneous errors of grammatical form.

The relationship between the different grammatical errors also deserves some notice. The astonishingly high rating of 1A (article errors) is of particular interest and could perhaps be taken to indicate that articles play a minor role in understanding; cf the results reported from Bradley (1970) in Section 1.5.7.[4] The rating of 2E (word-order errors) may seem to conflict with the rather lenient judgement of word-order errors in some previous experiments (Johansson 1975a: 34ff). However, most of the errors represented in 2E affected the order of major sentence constituents and differed from the error types studied previously.

Table 4:3 Experiment IV: mean ratings of texts containing different types of errors. A higher figure indicates a higher rating on the five-point scale (+5...1-). The figure in the righthand column specifies the rank of each version with respect to the other versions of the same text (from more, 1, to less acceptable). Test subjects: 25 university students.

Text	Mean rating	Rank
1A (incorrect choice of prepositions)	2.68	5
1B (spelling errors)	3.52	2
1C (lexical errors)	1.72	6
1D (concord errors)	3.28	3
1E (morphological errors)	2.80	4
1F (article errors)	4.36	1
2A (miscellaneous grammatical errors)	2.28	5
2B (lexical errors)	2.80	3
2C (spelling errors)	4.08	1
2D (lexical errors)	1.56	7
2E (word-order errors)	2.40	4
2F (lexical errors)	2.16	6
2G (morphological errors)	3.68	2

In conclusion, it should be pointed out that the versions containing spelling errors (1B and 2C) were judged very leniently, although they included errors such as hear for here and their for there. The rating of the spelling errors, as well as the mutual relationships between lexical and grammatical errors, conflicts sharply with the grading reported in the Appendix.

4.4 Grammatical vs lexical errors: discussion

Experiments III and IV agree in assigning a higher degree of irritation to lexical than to grammatical errors. This corresponds to the results of Engh (1971) and the cloze test research reported in Section 1.5.7. The fact that grammatical errors cause fewer problems of interpretation than do lexical ones is not surprising. By definition, grammar deals with the rule-governed, predictable aspects of language, the lexicon with the idiosyncratic, unpredictable aspects. A grammatical choice is part of a closed system, a lexical choice involves a selection from among members of an open class. In interpreting sentences with lexical errors the receiver is therefore faced with a more difficult task, since the possibilities of correction are much more varied and his knowledge of the language offers less help in predicting the correct form.[5]

Although Experiments III and IV agree in assigning a higher degree of irritation to lexical than to grammatical errors, this does not necessarily imply any criticism of the grading reported in the Appendix. As pointed out in another context (Section 1.3), a variety of principles must be taken into account in the evaluation of errors. According to one of these principles, generality, grammatical errors would be more serious than lexical errors. It could, however, be questioned whether the principle of generality has not often been given too much weight at the expense of the communicative principle.

The present investigation has only included a limited number of examples of lexical and grammatical deviance. There is a need for further studies with a wider range of errors. In particular, there is a need for more systematic surveys of the different types of deviance. Preferably, such studies should investigate not only <u>how</u> receivers react to particular cases of deviance but also <u>why</u> they react in the way they do.

NOTES

1 The order between the two texts in each test form was also varied such that every other participant received the texts in a different order.

2 Any words or phrases which closely approached the intended meaning were defined as "correct interpretations". Examples: is like or resembles for compares with, home or centre of production for headquarters, competitors or opponents for rivals. In one case main artery and veins were accepted as correct interpretations for backbone and ribs, respectively.

3 Test subjects received one test booklet at a time. The order of the booklets was alternated for every other test subject.

4 Bradley's finding that texts with deleted articles were understood better than the complete versions seems, however, questionable and needs further investigation.

5 There is, however, no doubt that certain grammatical errors would cause serious problems of interpretation, e g random scrambling of words or some of the cases of grammatical deviance taken up in the experiments reported in Section 1.5.6. The errors represented in this investigation differ from such cases of deviance in being actual errors that have been produced by language learners.

APPENDIX. EXPERIMENTS III, IV: MATERIAL

Text 1 Model translation:

There is nothing on earth that really compares with Fleet Street. This busy main street which runs like a backbone through the eastern part of central London with several side-streets like ribs on either side has been the home of the British press for more than three hundred years. The headquarters of many periodicals and weeklies are also situated here. In no other country is the press so "concentrated" as it is here, and nowhere else are the journalists so friendly to each other and at the same time such rivals. Things have gone so far that the name Fleet Street does not make one think primarily of a London street but of the noble art of journalism as such.

Text 1 Incorrect versions:

A (incorrect choice of prepositions):

1 resembles of for compares with (2)
5-6 in more than three hundred years for for more than... (3)
9 friendly against for friendly to (2)
10 on the same time for at the same time (2)
12 on the noble art for of the noble art (2)

B (spelling errors):

1 realy for really (2)
5 british for British (2)
7 weeklys for weeklies (2)
8 hear for here (2)
12 Londonstreet for London street (2)

C (lexical errors):

1 likes for compares with (3)
3 vertebra for backbone (2)
4 rapebones for ribs (2)
6 homage for headquarters (2)
10 concurrents for rivals (2)

D (concord errors):

1 compare for compares (3)
2 run for runs (3)
4 have for has (3)
7 is for are (3)
9 is for are (3)

E (morphological errors):

4 on each sides for on either side (3)
9 each others for each other (3)
10 have went for have gone (3)
12 primary for primarily (3)
12 the nobly art for the noble art (3)

F (article errors):

1 on the earth for on earth (2)
2 the Fleet Street for Fleet Street (3)
3 the central London for central London (2)
5 British press for the British press (2)
13 the journalism for journalism (2)

Text 2 Model translation:

Many people put the wrong books on their shelves or rather they do not have any principle about what they put there but fill their shelves with everything they have happened to get hold of. One should not put on one's shelves any other books than those one intends to read over again. The fact that a book is not worth reading more than once need not imply any criticism. Newspapers and weeklies are not usually read more than once either, however good they may be. It is always fun to look at other people's bookshelves. If one is interested in books, one can see straight away whether what is there is a genuine collection or only a row of beautiful bindings.

Text 2 Incorrect versions:

A (miscellaneous grammatical errors):

3 filling for fill (3)
4 with all what for with everything (3)
5-6 is thinking of to read for intends to read (3)
6-7 worth to be read for worth reading (3)
8 are not used to be read for are not usually read (3)

B (lexical errors):

1 strings for shelves (3)
3 " " "
5 " " "
10 bookstrings for bookshelves
12 what is on the strings for what is there

C (spelling errors):

2 principal for principle (2)
5 ones for one's (2)
10 peoples for people's (2)
12 their for there (3)
13 beatiful for beautiful (2)

D (lexical errors):

3 get over for get hold of (2)
7 ponder for criticism (2)
12 summon for collection (2)
13 raw for row (2)
13 bands for bindings (2)

E (word-order errors):

6 not is for is not (3)
8 Nor newspapers and weeklies are for Newspapers and weeklies are not... (3)
10-11 Is one interested for If one is interested (2)
11 can one for one can (3)
12 if it only is for [if it is] only (2)

F (lexical errors):

2 *princip* for *principle* (2)
4 *get catch of* for *get hold of* (2)
7 *critic* for *criticism* (2)
9 *fun* for *funny* (2)
11 *interesting* for *interested* (3)

G (morphological errors):

1 *shelfs* for *shelves* (3)
3 " " "
5 " " "
10 *bookshelfs* for *bookshelves*
12 *what is on the bookshelfs* for *what is there*

Note:

1 The incorrect versions can be derived from the model translations by inserting the words or expressions in the places specified.

2 The figure within parentheses after each error indicates how the error was graded (cf Section 4.2.1). Only the first occurrence of the error was marked in 2B and 2G.

5 Foreign Accent and Speech Distortion: Another Look [1]

5.1 Background

As reported in Section 1.5.1, Lane (1963) investigated reactions to foreign accent under varying conditions of masking and filtering. Foreign-accent speech was found to be approximately 40% less intelligible than native speech under all experimental conditions. It might, however, have been expected that the gap between understanding the foreigner and the native would grow wider with an increasing level of distortion. Such an interaction effect between linguistic deviance and mechanical distortion was found in Miller & Isard's (1963) study, where the gap between understanding grammatical and ungrammatical or semantically anomalous sentences increased with the level of distortion (though it narrowed again as the disturbance grew very severe). Expressed in another way, the deviant sentences were more sensitive to mechanical distortion than were the grammatical sentences.[2] Analogously, one would expect foreign-accent speech to be more sensitive to mechanical distortion than native speech. Experiment V was designed specifically to attempt to answer this question.

5.2 Experiment V

5.2.1 Material and method

One problem with Lane's (1963) experiment was that the material consisted entirely of monosyllables recorded without a context. It was therefore decided to use more natural material in Experiment V. Four texts (A, B, C, D) were selected. The texts were approximately the same length, 175-200 words, and dealt with similar subjects. Text A was recorded by a native speaker of English. Texts B, C. and D were recorded by three (different) native speakers and three foreigners.[3] The speakers were male and 25-40 years old. The natives were speakers of RP, or slightly modified RP. Two of the foreigners were Swedes who spoke English with a rather strong accent. The third was a Swede with an extensive experience of teaching English pronunciation who was asked to read the texts with a typical Swedish accent.[4] This arrangement was preferred, as it was difficult to find volunteers who both had representative accents and were willing to make the recordings.

A foreign version (Sw) was constructed for texts B, C, and D by selecting approximately one third of each text from each of the speakers. Native versions (Eng) were prepared in a corresponding manner. This procedure resulted in a foreign and a native version for each of the texts B, C, and D, i e six test passages. Two distorted versions (Dist 1 and Dist 2) were prepared for each of these test passages.[5] The distortion was produced by quantization. The speech signal was digitized and quantized in one and two bits, i e only two (Dist 2) and four (Dist 1) levels of the speech signal were used.[6] The quantizing levels were chosen so that noise was reduced.

Six groups of subjects listened to test tapes containing a different combination of passages in the order listed below:

	G1:	G2:	G3:	G4:	G5:	G6:
Undist	A	A	A	A	A	A
Undist	B_{Eng}	C_{Eng}	D_{Eng}	B_{Sw}	C_{Sw}	D_{Sw}
Dist 1	C_{Eng}	D_{Eng}	B_{Eng}	C_{Sw}	D_{Sw}	B_{Sw}
Dist 2	D_{Eng}	B_{Eng}	C_{Eng}	D_{Sw}	B_{Sw}	C_{Sw}

Text A was common to the six groups and was included partly as a practice passage, partly as a means of establishing the comparability of the groups. The test subjects were fourth-form school children from Lancaster and Preston: G1 (N: 25) and G4 (N: 24) from the Royal Grammar School, Lancaster; G2 (N: 25) and G5 (N: 23) from Ripley St Thomas Comprehensive School, Lancaster; G3 (N: 25) and G6 (N: 24) from Fulwood County High School, Preston.[7] Groups from the same school were matched and selected from corresponding ability sets. The groups from the Royal Grammar School in Lancaster consisted of boys only, the others were mixed. The subjects were 14-15 years old.

The tests were administered in an ordinary classroom using a Tandberg tape-recorder. They took approximately 25 minutes and were introduced as exercises in English classes. Test subjects were informed that they would listen to texts recorded by natives or foreigners, that the speaker might change in the middle of a passage, and that some of the recordings would be mechanically distorted and might be difficult to hear. They received a written answer sheet containing an incomplete version of the texts and were asked to fill in the missing portions. This is the procedure which has been termed partial dictation (Johansson 1975a: 123ff). There were 8-10 gaps of 3-9 words in each passage; these were the same in all the versions of the same text. In all, 50 words were left out in each text, i e about a fourth of the complete text. For each gap in the answer sheet, pauses had been inserted on the test tapes leaving the subjects ample time to write down the missing portions.

The tests administered to G1 and G4 were also given to two groups of Swedish school children. These were two equivalent groups enrolled in the first year of the "gymnasium" at Katedralskolan, Lund and will be termed G7 (N: 23) and G8 (N: 25).[8] The Swedish test subjects were 16-17 years old and had studied English for seven years.

5.2.2 Experiment V: results

The tests were scored according to the principles set forth in Johansson (1975a: 131f). 1 point was given for each word filled in correctly and in the right place by the test subject. This means a maximum score of 50 for each text. Spelling errors were disregarded provided that the words were clearly recognizable.

Likewise (and in contrast to the principles outlined in Johansson, 1975), errors in inflexional endings were disregarded, as it became obvious that these were frequently neglected. The scoring was carried out by the experimenter and was felt to be satisfactory, though there were occasional cases of hesitant judgement. To give an idea of the response types, a selection of responses is given in an Appendix.

The mean scores for texts B, C, and D are given in Tables 5:1 and 5:2. Before we examine these, it is important to study the scores for text A which was common to all the groups:

G1: 48.56	G4: 47.82	G7: 28.17
G2: 43.95	G5: 44.73	G8: 28.96
G3: 45.92	G6: 46.16	
$Mean_{G1-3}$: 46.14	$Mean_{G4-6}$: 46.24	

The results for text A are thus closely comparable for all the groups whose scores we are interested in comparing, i e G1 and G4, G2 and G5, G3 and G6, G7 and G8. These groups were from the same schools and listened to the same combination of test passages, though one heard native and the other foreign versions of texts B, C, and D; cf Section 5.2.1.

Table 5:1 shows that the gap between the native's understanding of foreigners and other natives is rather small under undistorted conditions but grows appreciably wider under conditions of distortion. This is more clearly brought out in Fig 5:1, where the mean scores are plotted for all the foreign vs all the native text versions under undistorted and distorted conditions. The scores were, however, more or less the same for the two conditions of distortion.

The results for the two Swedish listener groups, which are given in Table 5:2 and are also plotted in Fig 5:1, differ in several respects from those of the native listeners. As is to be expected, the scores for the Swedes were much lower under all conditions. More importantly, the overall picture of the results

Table 5:1 Experiment V: mean perception scores for texts read by natives and foreigners, distorted and undistorted. English listeners: G1 (N: 25) and G4 (N:24), Royal Grammar School, Lancaster; G2 (N: 25) and G5 (N:23), Ripley St Thomas Comprehensive School, Lancaster; G3 (N: 25) and G6 (N: 24), Fulwood County High School, Preston. Maximum score per text: 50.

	Native speakers				Foreign speakers			
Conditions	Text B	Text C	Text D	Mean	Text B	Text C	Text D	Mean
Undist	G1: 49.72	G2: 49.36	G3: 48.32	G1-3: 49.13	G4: 47.41	G5: 45.39	G6: 46.70	G4-6: 46.50
Dist 1	G3: 45.68	G1: 48.24	G2: 43.48	G1-3: 45.80	G6: 39.42	G4: 43.29	G5: 32.04	G4-6: 38.25
Dist 2	G2: 42.88	G3: 45.48	G1: 47.56	G1-3: 45.31	G5: 31.87	G6: 38.33	G4: 42.58	G4-6: 37.60

Table 5:2 Experiment V: mean perception scores for texts read by natives and foreigners, distorted and undistorted. Swedish listeners: G7 (N: 23) and G8 (N: 25), Katedralskolan, Lund. Maximum score per text: 50.

Conditions	Native speakers (G7)	Foreign speakers (G8)
Undist	Text B: 35.65	Text B: 36.92
Dist 1	Text C: 25.30	Text C: 27.12
Dist 2	Text D: 23.09	Text D: 21.68

Fig 5:1 Experiment V: perception scores for texts read by natives and foreigners, distorted and undistorted. English and Swedish listeners. Cf Tables 5:1 and 5:2.

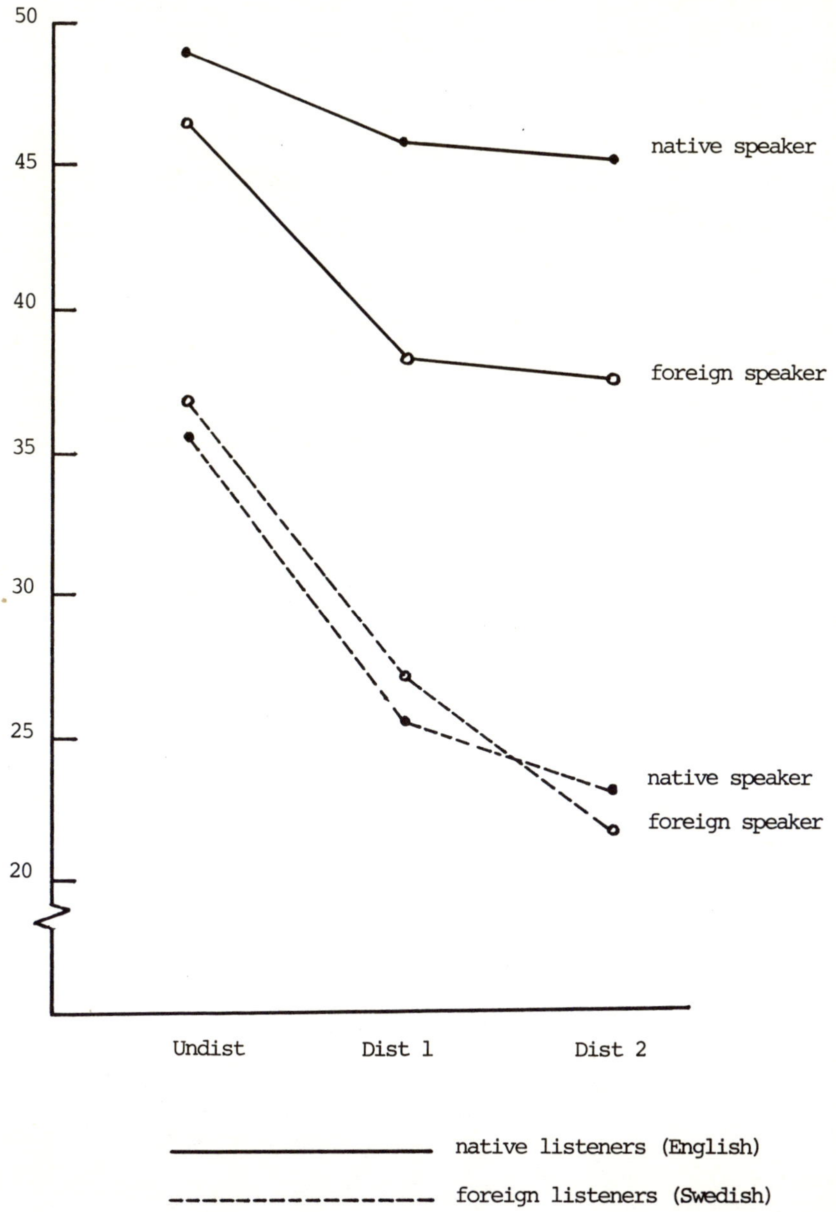

is completely different. There was no appreciable difference between the foreigner's understanding of natives and other foreigners with the same native-language background. Finally, the foreign listeners showed a greater sensitivity to mechanical distortion, as evidenced by the scores under the two conditions of distortion. The scores for the foreign listeners in the latter case are, however, somewhat uncertain, as the scoring system outlined above is less satisfactory when the partial dictation is very incompletely or inaccurately filled in.

5.3 Foreign accent and speech distortion: discussion

Experiment V does not give a complete answer to the question of the relationship between foreign accent and speech distortion. It was unexpected that the scores for the native listeners were more or less the same under the two levels of distortion. This is probably due to adaptation to the distorted situation, since it is well-known that listening to distorted speech improves with practice (Licklider & Miller 1951: 1068; cf also Johansson 1975a: 168). Such an adaptation effect would then counter-balance an increase in the level of distortion.

The experiment shows clearly that foreign-accent speech, when perceived by the native, is more sensitive to mechanical distortion than is native speech. The gap between understanding the native and the foreigner, which was rather small under undistorted conditions, grew appreciably wider under the two conditions of distortion. This demonstrates the need to eliminate features of foreign accent, even though they may seem unimportant under optimal circumstances. Spoken communication is often disturbed in various ways, and it is therefore necessary to keep up a certain level of redundancy to ensure success of communication. The following chapter will tackle the problem of grading specific features of foreign accent according to the reactions of groups of native listeners.

Before leaving the subject of the native listeners' reactions, it should be pointed out that there were wide differences between test subjects from the different schools; see Table 5:1 (cf also the scores for text A given in Section 5.2.2). The highest results occurred in G1 and G4 (grammar school), the lowest in G2 and G5 (comprehensive school). The largest differences occurred with the foreign speakers under distorted conditions. These results show the need to take the type of receiver into account in studies of native reactions to learners' errors; cf Section 1.4.

The greater sensitivity to distortion of foreign-accent speech applies only to the native listeners. As pointed out in the preceding section, there was a completely different reaction among the foreign listeners, who understood the foreigners about as well as the natives under all experimental conditions. This result was expected. It was hypothesized that a foreigner's comprehension of other foreigners with the same native-language background would be equal to, or even surpass, his comprehension of native speakers. This seems natural, as the foreigner would be just as familiar, or even more familiar, with this type of foreign-accent speech than with native speech. Such a reaction would also follow naturally from the normally slower speed of delivery of foreign-accent speech.[9] The results confirm the hypothesis and would perhaps have been even clearer with a slightly more advanced group of foreign listeners.[10]

In conclusion, it should be pointed out that, even though the natives had difficulties in understanding foreign-accent speech under distorted conditions, the ability to tolerate distortion was smaller among the foreign listeners (cf the preceding section, the end). This agrees with general observations on differences between natives and foreigners in their ability to understand speech under disturbed conditions; cf the references in Johansson 1975a: 101ff.

NOTES

1 The experiment reported in this chapter was stimulated by a suggestion made by Professor Björn Lindblom at the Symposium on Phonetics and the Teaching of Pronunciation in Stockholm, May 1975.

2 A similar effect appeared in a study of "semantically well and semantically poorly integrated sentences" by Rosenberg & Jarvella (1970). Both types of sentences were perceived equally well under quiet conditions, but the presence of noise produced a difference in favour of the semantically well integrated sentences.

3 The recording took place in an echo-free room on a Studer A62 tape-recorder using a Sennheiser MD421 microphone. The recording speed was 7.5 i.p.s.

4 This Swedish speaker was identical to the speaker who recorded the material of Experiment VI. See the following chapter.

5 The distorted versions were produced by Rolf Carlsson and Björn Granström at the Royal Institute of Technology, Stockholm.

6 For a description of quantization, see Cherry (1966: 47ff, 172ff).

7 I am grateful to the staff at these schools for assistance in administering the tests, in particular to Mr Alan Newton at the Royal Grammar School in Lancaster, Mrs Haynes at Ripley St Thomas Comprehensive School in Lancaster, and Mr Michael Jacob at Fulwood County High School in Preston.

8 I am indebted to fil mag Jesper Wetterberg for administering the tests at Katedralskolan, Lund.

9 The speed of delivery was, in fact, considerably slower in the recordings made by the foreigners in Experiment V.

10 A study of responses shows that the texts were too difficult for the two groups of foreign listeners, who were unfamiliar with some of the vocabulary.

APPENDIX. EXPERIMENT V: EXAMPLES OF RESPONSES

Short extracts from the original text are given with the portions to be filled in by test subjects underlined. Examples of responses are given below the underlined portions. All the extracts have been taken from text B, which deals with "A Day in the Life of a British Ambassador".

His rooms are the <u>heart of the embassy</u>.
mark of the embassy
part of the embassy
property of the embassy
rear of the embassy
best in the Embassy
enclosed in the embassy
heart of the ambassador
mark of the ambassador
best for an ambassador
of the best quality
ones at the top of the building

... by ten o'clock he must be <u>ready to meet his chief assistants</u>
ready to meet his chief resident(s)/
president(s)/representatives/
ambassador/solicitor/visitors/
ministers/executive
ready to leave his key president
able to meet his chief president
able to meet his chief residents

... for <u>there is no sex-barrier nowadays</u> in the British Foreign Service
there is no seats for young nowadays
there is no sex nowadays
no experience these days
there is no seats nowadays
there is no pay nowadays
there is no time our days
there is no sex order these days
there is no safe career nowadays
there is no such barrier
there is a meeting
associates in our days
instance nowadays
there is no sex carried out nowadays

... discuss the problems <u>arising in their different fields</u>
arising in the country
arising in the area that week
arising in the different states
arising in the area of fields
arising in their different feats
arising in the indignant speech
that have arisen
there arises in the arrogant peace
facing the government
that they referred to that case
of racing in very different fields
the racing in different fields
racing in their industrious fear
erasing their different views
erasing in the very different fields
raised in the different beat
there is in indignant speech
there is a different heat
there are India and roundabouts
relating to there
on their differences
of a nurse lying in the fields

... from his <u>wider experience and knowledge of his government's policy</u>
wide/vital/worldwide/rather/other/life/great/later/
prior/point experience...
vital experience and knowledge of this government policy
wider experience and knowledge of this government position
wider experience and knowledge of his government theory
other experience and knowledge of his cabinet for instance
wide experience he can do what is right
experience he does what the government allows
wide experience and knowledge of this policy
vital experience and help he has from governance policy
point of experience and notes from his government policy
great experience and knowledge of the government
vital knowledge and no all of his government policy
riding experience and from his government policy

6 Types of Phonological Errors

6.1 Background

Phonological errors have been dealt with previously in the investigation. The preceding chapter was concerned with the general effect of a deviant pronunciation. Experiment I, which was reported in Chapter 2, contained examples of different kinds of phonological errors, but the material was too small to allow any safe conclusions about differences in reactions due to the kind of phonological deviance. A series of experiments was therefore designed to tackle especially this problem.

6.2 Experiment VI: types of segmental errors

6.2.1 Material and method

12 groups of 2-4 sentences were recorded by a Swede who speaks excellent English (Received Pronunciation) but is also very familiar with pronunciation problems typical of Swedish students of English.[1] The speaker was instructed to "fake" particular kinds of pronunciation errors in the sentences. The material is listed in Table 6:1. The errors included were, with one exception (the last sentence in group 9), segmental and were such errors as might occur among Swedish students of English. Correct versions were also recorded in four cases (groups 4, 5, 11, 12).

The sentences were placed in random order, with the exception that members of the same group were never placed in immediate succession. The ordering is given in Table 6:1. 6 sentences were copied (from groups 2, 6, 7, 8, 9, 10) and placed at the beginning or end of the test. The test items were separated by a pause of 3-4 seconds.

The test tape was played in a language laboratory to a group of 23 university students at the University of Lancaster, who had taken part in Experiment I on a previous occasion. The subjects were 18-20 years old; 17 were male, 6 female. All except

Table 6:1 Experiment VI: results. The figure within parentheses before each test item indicates its order in the test. The scores given state the mean rating assigned by test subjects on a five-point scale of acceptability (+5...1-). Test subjects: 23 university students.

Group		Test items	Mean rating
1	(20)	There was an explosion /iks'pləuʃən/ near the station.	2.70
	(5)	There was an explosion near the station /'steiʒən/.	2.57
2	(22)	They visited Land's End /ænd/.	3.70
	(2, 39)	They visited Land's /lendz/ End.	3.26, 3.26
	(12)	They visited /'visitid/ Land's End.	3.04
3	(26)	Let's sing something /'sʌmsiŋ/ else.	3.09
	(32)	Let's sing (pronounced with a close Swedish /i/) ...	4.09
	(24)	Let's sing something else (with clear /l/).	3.48
4	(31)	There was /wəs/ ice on the road.	3.09
	(19)	There was ice /aiz/ on the road.	2.00
	(17)	There was ice on the road. (correct)	3.87
5	(36)	Mr Wilson is a writer ['raitə].	3.70
	(11)	Mr Wilson is a writer ['Raitə].	2.57
	(21)	Mr Wilson is a writer ['ɹaitəɹ].	3.96
	(15)	Mr Wilson is a writer. (correct)	4.35
6	(35)	Some people don't like (with dark /l/) milk.	4.35
	(6, 40)	Some people (with clear /l/) don't like milk.	4.13, 3.96
	(16)	Some people don't like milk (with clear /l/).	3.83
7	(7)	This boat is very cheap /ʃi:p/.	1.96
	(3, 34)	This boat [bo:t] is very cheap.	3.48, 3.39
	(37)	This boat [bæut] is very cheap.	2.87
8	(9)	This is /is/ Miss Jones /dʒəuns/.	3.26
	(1, 29)	This /ðiz/ is Miss /miz/ Jones.	2.61, 2.74
	(13)	This is [iz:] Miss Jones [dʒəunz:].	3.57
9	(14)	Ted /tæd/ is interested in politics.	4.22
	(18, 42)	Ted is /is/ interested in politics.	3.35, 3.00
	(30)	Ted is interested in politics /pə'litiks/.	2.39
10	(4, 41)	John is a young /dʒʌŋ/ architect.	2.17, 1.83
	(8)	John /jɔn/ is a young architect.	2.09
	(28)	John is a yong architect /'ɑ:tʃitekt/.	2.13
11	(27)	Sarah sings very well /vel/.	1.83
	(23)	Sarah sings very /'weri/ well.	2.04
	(38)	Sarah sings very well. (correct)	4.26
12	(33)	They don't want to do /dəu/ it.	3.30
	(25)	They /dei/ don't want to do it.	3.57
	(10)	They don't want to do it. (correct)	4.57

two were enrolled in non-language subjects. They were all from the United Kingdom, though their place of origin varied widely.[2] The majority had not spent more than a month in a foreign country, nor had they had much contact with foreigners in England. The subjects received the following instructions:

You will hear a foreigner pronounce a series of English sentences. The same sentences appear several times in the test. Your task is to grade the pronunciation of each sentence using a five-point scale:

native-like pronunciation + — — — — — - strong foreign accent

Listen carefully now and grade each item by putting a mark on the scale provided. There will be a pause of 3-4 seconds between each item and a slightly longer pause as you turn the page.

Each subject received an answer sheet containing a written version of each test item, followed by a scale of the type specified in the instructions.

6.2.2 Experiment VI: results

The results have been summarized in detail in Table 6:1. First, it should be noted that the scores for repeated items show only slight differences (0.00, 0.17, 0.09, 0.13, 0.35, 0.34). It therefore seems justified to draw safe conclusions from the results. Second, it should be noted that the four correct recordings (in groups 4, 5, 11, 12) received considerably higher scores than the other members in the same group (a difference from the next highest score of 0.78, 0.39, 2.22, 1.00, respectively). The testing method therefore seems to have worked satisfactorily. The fact that none of the correct versions received the maximum score should not disturb us. This is rather to be expected due to the differences in dialectal background of the listeners (cf note 2).

We shall now examine the results in greater detail. The discussion will be based on both intra-group and inter-group comparisons. Note, however, that the latter type of comparison is less reliable, due to the difference in lexical material between the groups. On the other hand, the scores for sentences in the same group could be compared more safely, as a major difference in scores could only be related to the difference in error type.

6.2.2.1 Phonemic vs subphonemic errors

It is frequently argued that errors involving the substitution of one phoneme for another are more serious than subphonemic errors, as the former may cause misunderstandings whereas the latter only give rise to a deviant accent without affecting comprehensibility.[3] The results of Experiment VI do indeed show that native speakers often judge phonemic errors to be more serious. This appears in the three cases where phonemic and subphonemic errors were contrasted in the same group:

Group 3: The substitution of /s/ for /θ/ in <u>something</u> received a lower score than <u>sing</u> pronounced with a close /i/ and <u>else</u> pronounced with a clear /l/.

Group 7: The substitution of /ʃ/ for /tʃ/ in <u>cheap</u> received a lower score than deviant (i e with respect to RP) realizations of the vowel in <u>boat</u>.

Group 8: The substitution of /s/ for /z/, and vice versa, received lower scores than /z/ realized with strong "buzzing".

The greater severity of many phonemic errors is also shown by inter-group comparison; note e g the low scores for the phonemic errors in groups 1, 7, 10, 11 and the high scores for subphonemic errors in groups 3, 5, 6. Nevertheless, the difference in acceptability between the two types of phonological deviance is far from consistent. A phonemic error sometimes received fairly high scores:

Groups 2, 9: The use of /æ/ for /e/ in *Land's End* received the score 3.70, whereas the opposite substitution was judged to be less acceptable. The substitution of /æ/ for /e/ in *Ted* received an extremely high score, 4.22.

Group 12: The substitution of /əu/ for /u:/ in *do* received the score 3.30.

Groups 3, 12: The substitution of /s/ for /θ/ in *something* and, especially, /d/ for /ð/ in *they* received higher ratings than might have been expected (3.09 and 3.57, respectively).

Groups 2, 4, 8, 9: The substitution of /s/ for /z/ received scores around or above 3 (3.04, 3.09, 3.26, 3.35, 3.00). The opposite substitution was, however, judged to be more severe; cf Section 6.2.2.3.

Certain subphonemic errors received lower ratings than the phonemic errors just mentioned:

Group 5: The realization of the initial consonant in *writer* as [R] received the score 2.57.

Group 7: The use of [æu] in *boat* received a fairly low score, 2.87.

Experiment VI therefore illustrates that the relationship between phonemic and subphonemic errors is by no means simple.[4]

The higher acceptability of certain phonemic errors, e g the substitution of /æ/ for /e/, is clearly related to the existence of variations of pronunciation within the English-speaking community. Gimson (1970: 104) reports that /e/ has a quality close to the cardinal vowel [ɛ] in some kinds of RP and many regional dialects. Similarly, the rather high acceptability of /əu/ for /u:/ in do may be due to the existence of diphthongized variants of this vowel (Gimson 1970: 120). There are probably also other reasons for the rather high acceptability values of certain phonemic errors. The surprisingly high values for the substitution of /s/ for /θ/ in something and /d/ for /ð/ in they must partially be due to the unstressed position of the consonants. The same might partially explain the rather high scores for the substitution of /s/ for /z/, though the frequent occurrence of devoicing of /z/ must also be taken into account (see the following section).

It is thus possible to explain why the acceptability rating varies with different phonemic substitutions. The variation among subphonemic errors can be explained along the same lines. The subphonemic deviance (with respect to RP) in the realization of /l/ and /r/ is clearly rated differently due to the existence of pronunciation variants within the English-speaking community. Hence, an "incorrect" distribution of clear and dark /l/ and the pronunciation of /r/ in final position or the realization of /r/ as an apical trill received high scores (groups 5 and 6), as these features are frequent among native speakers of English. On the other hand, the realization of /r/ as [R] is given a much lower rating than the other variants in group 5, as a uvular [R] is only used by a small section of the English-speaking community and appears, in addition, to be on the decrease (Påhlsson 1972). The difference in scores between the two realizations of /əu/ in group 7 should perhaps be explained in the same way. Both [o:] and [æu] are found among native speakers of English (cf Gimson 1970: 132f), but the former realization is no doubt more widespread.

The degree of severity of phonemic and subphonemic errors is therefore above all related to the existence of variations among native speakers of English. If an "error" is identical to a pronunciation which is widespread among native speakers of English, it is judged to be more acceptable. On the other hand, completely non-native deviations, whether phonemic or subphonemic, are given low acceptability ratings. It should, however, be pointed out that the mere existence of variations may not be a sufficient factor. In addition, the social prestige of different pronunciation variants must be taken into account.[5] This factor might explain why the substitution of /æ/ for /e/ is rated better than the substitution of /əu/ for /u:/ or why there is a considerable difference in acceptability rating between the two realizations of /əu/.

Apart from the factors already taken up, there are probably also more general factors of perceptual distance which might explain varying reactions to different phonemic and subphonemic deviations. The material is, however, too small to allow any definite conclusions in this respect. A more extensive study of reactions in tests of the kind represented by Experiment VI could perhaps yield relevant information for establishing a hierarchy of phonetic differences.

6.2.2.2 The direction of phonemic substitutions

The material presented in the preceding section shows that the acceptability of phonemic substitutions may vary. We shall now take up a specific problem of this kind, viz the question whether there is a difference in acceptability rating depending on the direction of error in a particular phonemic contrast. Is the reaction to the substitution /x/→/y/ identical to or different from that of the opposite substitution, i e /y/→/x/? A study of the material, based on intra-group comparison, reveals that there is no clear answer.

Group 1: The substitution of /ʃ/ for /ʒ/ and /ʒ/ for /ʃ/ received approximately the same rating.

Group 2: The substitution of /æ/ for /e/ was judged to be more acceptable than the opposite substitution, /e/ for /æ/.

Groups 4, 8: The substitution of /s/ for /z/ was judged to be more acceptable than the opposite substitution, /z/ for /s/.

Group 10: The substitution of /j/ for /dʒ/ and /dʒ/ for /j/ received approximately the same rating.

Group 11: The substitution of /v/ for /w/ and /w/ for /v/ received approximately the same rating.

Two cases thus show clear differences, whereas the rest were hardly affected by the direction of substitution.

A difference in acceptability might be expected depending on whether the phonemic error is an example of underdifferentiation or hypercorrection. However, these two types of errors were treated indiscriminately in several cases, e g /'veri 'vel/ and /'weri 'wel/ for very well in group 11. There must therefore be other reasons why the acceptability rating varies sometimes depending on the direction of substitution. The two cases which occur in the material should probably be explained in different ways.

Group 2: The higher acceptability of the substitution of /æ/ for /e/, as compared with /e/ for /æ/ , is probably due to the widespread realization of /e/ as a rather open vowel (cf the preceding section), whereas a closer realization of /æ/ is less common.

Groups 4, 8: The non-symmetric relationship between /s/ and /z/ is probably due to the normal direction of assimilation in English. /z/ is frequently devoiced, with the lenis

> character preserved (Gimson 1970: 179); in addition, complete assimilation /z/→/s/ may occur at word and morpheme boundaries. The opposite type of assimilation, i e voiceless→ voiced, is not characteristic of English (Gimson 1970: 294).

Note, finally, that there was a slight difference in acceptability depending on the direction of substitution in group 1 (/ʃ/ and /ʒ/). The relationship between acceptability and the direction of substitution was comparable to that of /s/ and /z/.

6.2.2.3 Vowel and consonant errors

It is possible that there is a difference in acceptability between vowel and consonant errors. It could be argued on general grounds that vowels should be less sensitive to errors than consonants. Gimson (1970: 4) points out that "we can replace our twenty English vowels by the single vowel [ə] in any utterance and still, if the rhythmic pattern is kept, retain a high degree of intelligibility". A similar reduction of acoustic information in the case of consonants would certainly make most utterances incomprehensible.

The material in Experiment VI is insufficient to allow any safe conclusions concerning possible differences between vowel and consonant errors. Note, however, that several consonant errors received extremely low ratings (around 2), whereas the lowest rating for a vowel error was just below 3 (2.87). It would be of interest to examine if this tendency would appear in an examination of a larger material.

6.3 Experiment VII: types of subphonemic errors

As shown in Experiment VI, the gravity of phonemic as well as subphonemic errors varies depending on the type of deviance. Though phonemic errors are normally judged to be more severe, this is by no means without exceptions. Other factors, especially the existence of variations of pronunciation within the English-speaking community, will also have to be taken into account. Subphonemic errors which represent completely non-native realizations may be more serious than certain phonemic errors. This is hardly surprising. The listener must not only be able to discriminate between phonemes; he must also be able to assign phonetic realizations to the intended phonemic category. The latter task could be endangered by deviant realizations.

Experiment VII was designed to establish a scale of gravity for subphonemic errors which may result from the substitution of Swedish sounds in the pronunciation of English. The investigation is a continuation of a previous study of a similar kind (Johansson 1975a: 60ff).

6.3.1 Material and method

As in the previous study the method involved an investigation of how native speakers of English react to S[wedish] words presented as E[nglish]. A series of Swedish-English test pairs was constructed; see Table 6:2. Most of the material consisted of groups of words exhibiting a minimal contrast, e g S <u>bi</u>, <u>bo</u>, etc, E <u>be</u>, <u>boo</u>, etc, S <u>batt</u>, <u>back</u>, E <u>but</u>, <u>buck</u>. S and E sounds were contrasted in the neighbourhood of sounds which had previously been found to be identical or very similar. Much of the S material consisted of nonsense words, whereas the E material contained only actually occurring E words. Note, especially, that two of the S words (26 and 30) contained S consonants in unusual positions.

The S words were recorded, in the order listed in Table 6:2, by 16 Swedish speakers.[6] The speakers were instructed to read each word by itself, with a pause of 2-3 seconds between each, and without varying the intonation pattern.[7] Most of the speakers were students of phonetics or English at Lund University; additional information on the speakers is given in Appendix I.

The word lists, after the recordings had been edited and pauses adjusted, were played in a language laboratory to groups of students at the University of Lancaster. The test subjects had previously taken part in either Experiment I or Experiment VI, or both. They were 18-24 years old. The majority were male students enrolled in non-language subjects. Most of them had not spent more than a month in a foreign country, nor had they had much contact with foreigners in England. Regional background varied widely, though all participants were from the United Kingdon.[8] The listeners were divided into two groups (see Table 6:2), who took part in two test sessions each. Each group listened to eight speakers, in the order listed in the table, four at each test session. The following instructions were given:

You will hear a list of English words pronounced by foreigners. Your task is to grade the pronunciation of each word using a five-point scale:

native-like pronunciation	+	— — — — —	-	strong foreign accent

Listen carefully now and grade each item by putting a mark on the scale provided. Each word is separated by a pause of 2-3 seconds and a slightly longer pause is inserted after each column on the answer sheet.

Each participant received an answer sheet for each speaker containing two columns of English words (the English target words listed in Table 6:2) followed by scales of the type specified in the instructions.

6.3.2 Experiment VII: results

Experiment VII was designed to overcome some serious shortcomings in the previous study, especially as regards the choice of test words and the number of speakers (cf Johansson 1975a: 81). Note, however, that there were several other differences between the two investigations. First, the present study contained only S words recorded by Swedes, whereas the previous one also included E words recorded by native speakers of English. Second,

Table 6:2 Experiment VII: results. Test subjects: 42 university students. The results indicate the judgements by test subjects on a five-point scale of acceptability. Explanations:

+ more than half of the listeners indicated one of the two highest levels on the five-point scale
– " " " " " " " " " " " lowest " " " " "
? less " " " " " " " " " " highest or lowest levels on the five-point scale
Ø the test word was not pronounced by the speaker in question

Item	Swedish test word	English target	Listener group A (23) Swedish speakers 1	2	3	4	5	6	7	8	Total +	?	–	Listener group B (19) Swedish speakers 9	10	11	12	13	14	15	16	Total +	?	–	Groups A and B +	?	–
1	bi /bi:/	be	+	+	–	?	–	+	?	–	3	2	3	+	–	+	+	?	?	?	–	3	3	2	6	5	5
2	bo /bu:/	boo	+	?	?	?	–	–	?	?	1	5	2	?	–	–	?	+	?	–	–	1	3	4	2	8	6
3	bå /bo:/	bore	?	?	?	+	?	–	–	+	2	4	2	–	?	?	?	–	?	?	?	0	6	2	2	10	4
4	ba /bɑ:/	bar	?	+	+	?	+	–	?	+	4	3	1	+	+	+	?	–	+	?	+	5	2	1	9	5	2
5	bö /bø:/	burr	–	+	?	–	–	?	+	?	2	3	3	–	–	+	?	–	–	–	?	1	2	5	3	5	8
6	bäj /bɛj/	bay	–	+	–	?	+	+	?	+	4	2	2	+	?	+	–	?	?	?	?	2	5	1	6	7	3
7	baj /baj/	by	?	+	?	+	+	+	+	+	6	2	0	+	+	+	?	+	+	+	?	6	2	0	12	4	0
8	boj /bɔj/	boy	+	+	+	+	+	+	+	+	8	0	0	+	+	+	?	+	+	?	+	6	2	0	14	2	0
9	binn /bin/	bin	?	?	–	–	?	?	+	+	2	4	2	+	–	+	+	?	?	?	?	3	4	1	5	8	3
10	bänn /bɛn/	Ben	+	+	+	+	+	+	+	+	8	0	0	+	+	+	+	+	+	+	+	8	0	0	16	0	0
11	bänn /bɛn/	ban	–	–	–	–	–	–	–	–	0	0	8	–	–	–	–	–	–	–	–	0	0	8	0	0	16
12	bann /ban/	bun	+	+	+	+	+	+	+	+	8	0	0	+	+	+	+	+	+	+	+	8	0	0	16	0	0
13	bass /bas/	bus	+	?	+	+	+	+	+	+	7	1	0	+	+	+	?	+	+	+	+	7	1	0	14	2	0
14	puss /pʊs/	puss	+	+	+	?	+	–	?	+	5	2	1	?	?	?	?	+	?	?	+	2	6	0	7	8	1
15	/pUs/	puss	?	–	–	–	?	–	?	?	0	4	4	?	–	?	?	–	?	?	?	0	6	2	0	10	6
16	båss /bɔs/	boss	?	?	?	?	+	?	?	+	2	6	0	–	+	?	?	?	?	?	+	2	5	1	4	11	1
17	värn [væ:ɳ]	van	Ø	+	+	+	+	Ø	Ø	+	5	0	0	+	+	+	+	+	Ø	Ø	+	6	0	0	11	0	0
18	hem /hɛm/[9]	hem	+	+	+	+	+	+	+	+	8	0	0	+	+	+	+	?	–	–	+	5	1	2	13	1	2
19	hem /hɛm/	him	–	–	–	–	?	–	–	–	0	1	7	–	–	–	–	–	+	?	–	1	1	6	1	2	13

'able 6:2 (cont.)

tem	Swedish test word	English target	Listener group A (23) Swedish speakers 1	2	3	4	5	6	7	8	Total +	?	-	Listener group B (19) Swedish speakers 9	10	11	12	13	14	15	16	Total +	?	-	Groups A and B +	?	-
20	örn [œ:ɳ]	earn	Ø	-	?	+	+	Ø	Ø	+	3	1	1	+	?	+	?	+	Ø	Ø	?	3	3	0	6	4	1
21	sinn /sin/	sin	?	?	-	-	+	?	?	+	2	4	2	+	?	?	+	?	?	-	?	2	5	1	4	9	3
22	sinn /sin/	seen	-	-	+	+	-	?	-	-	2	1	5	-	-	-	-	-	-	?	-	0	1	7	2	2	12
23	bot /bu:/	boot	?	-	-	-	-	-	-	-	0	1	7	?	-	?	-	?	?	-	-	0	4	4	0	5	11
24	bort [bu:ʈ]	boot	Ø	?	-	Ø	-	Ø	Ø	-	0	1	3	?	-	-	?	?	Ø	Ø	-	0	3	3	0	4	6
25	taj /taj/	tie	?	+	?	+	?	?	+	?	3	5	0	+	?	+	?	+	+	?	-	4	3	1	7	8	1
26	[ʈaj]	tie	Ø	+	+	Ø	+	Ø	Ø	+	4	0	0	-	+	Ø	+	?	Ø	Ø	?	2	2	1	6	2	1
27	sjaj /ʃaj/[10]	shy	-	+	+	-	+	-	-	+	4	0	4	+	+	-	+	-	-	-	-	3	0	5	7	0	9
28	tjaj /çaj/	shy	?	+	?	+	+	+	+	+	6	2	0	-	-	+	+	+	+	?	?	4	2	2	10	4	2
29	hasch /haʃ/[11]	hush	-	?	+	-	+	-	-	+	3	1	4	+	+	-	+	-	-	-	+	4	0	4	7	1	8
30	hatj /haç/	hush	+	?	-	?	+	+	+	+	5	2	1	+	-	+	-	+	+	+	+	6	0	2	11	2	3
31	säll /sɛl/	sell	+	+	?	?	?	+	+	+	5	3	0	?	?	+	+	?	+	?	+	4	4	0	9	7	0
32	läss /lɛs/	less	+	+	+	+	+	+	+	+	8	0	0	+	+	+	+	+	+	+	+	8	0	0	16	0	0
33	gäss /jɛs/	yes	+	+	+	+	+	+	+	+	8	0	0	+	+	+	+	+	+	+	+	8	0	0	16	0	0
34	app /ap/	up	+	+	+	+	+	+	+	+	8	0	0	+	+	+	+	+	+	+	?	7	1	0	15	1	0
35	batt /bat/	but	+	+	?	+	?	?	+	+	5	3	0	+	+	?	?	+	+	+	?	5	3	0	10	6	0
36	back /bak/[12]	buck	?	?	-	?	-	?	?	?	0	6	2	?	?	?	?	?	?	?	-	0	7	1	0	13	3
37	rann /ran/	run	-	-	-	-	?	-	-	-	0	1	7	?	-	-	?	?	-	-	-	0	3	5	0	4	12
38	zink /sink/	sink	-	-	-	-	?	-	-	?	0	2	6	?	?	-	?	-	?	?	?	0	6	2	0	8	8
39	aj /aj/	eye	+	+	?	+	+	+	+	+	7	1	0	?	+	+	?	?	+	?	?	3	5	0	10	6	0
40	sitt /sit/	sit	?	?	-	-	?	-	?	?	0	5	3	?	?	?	?	-	?	?	?	0	7	1	0	12	4
41	pann /pan/	pun	+	+	+	+	+	+	+	+	8	0	0	+	?	?	+	+	+	+	?	5	3	0	13	3	0
42	bass /bas/	buzz	-	-	-	-	-	-	-	-	0	0	8	-	-	-	-	-	-	-	-	0	0	8	0	0	16

the task required of test subjects was quite different; in the present case, to give an acceptability judgement; in the previous case, to identify the speaker as a foreigner or a native. Third, the dialectal background of the listeners was mixed in the present investigation (cf the preceding section), whereas test subjects formed homogeneous groups in the previous study. Due to these and other differences, complete agreement could not be expected between the results of the two investigations.

The results of Experiment VII have been summarized in Table 6:2. In order to avoid giving a spurious impression of exactness, the reactions of the listeners have been converted to a three-point scale (+. ?, -). The results reveal, as was to be expected, that there may be wide differences in reaction to test words depending upon the Swedish speaker. Establishing a scale of gravity for subphonemic errors due to interference is therefore a difficult, if not impossible, task. The present study does not claim to give any definite answer, as there are too many uncertain factors involved. Apart from the difference of speakers, we must also consider the varying dialectal background of the listeners. For these reasons, the information in Table 6:2 could only be regarded as a starting-point for further, more detailed and more strictly controlled, studies.

Experiment VII illustrates a dilemma for the contrastive phonologist. Either he refines too much and ignores the existence of internal variation within the source and target language, and then the results are not generally applicable, or he mixes dialects as in this study, but then it is difficult to make general contrastive statements due to coincidental matching of the dialects of the source and target language.

In spite of the difficulties mentioned, some details deserve special notice. These will be briefly taken up in the following sections. Before we look at these details, it should just be pointed out that the testing method seems to have worked satisfactorily. There was fairly good agreement between similar test items occurring in different parts of the test (e g 12 and 41, 9 and 21, 7 and 39). Moreover, the test subjects seem to have accepted the testing situation as presented. They were surprised to hear at the end of the test that none of the words they had listened to were English.

6.3.2.1 Vowels and diphthongs

In most of the test pairs where E target vowels or diphthongs were contrasted with possible S equivalents, the rating varied considerably depending upon the speaker. There was, however, one case where a S test word was consistently rejected (11: S *bänn* for E *ban*).[13] On the other hand, there was complete, or almost complete, acceptance in the following cases:

7: S *baj* for E *by* (cf also 39)
8: S *boj* for E *boy*
10: S *bänn* for E *Ben* (cf also 18, 32, 33)
12: S *bann* for E *bun* (cf also 13, 34, 41)
17: S *värn* for E *van*

In a few other cases, test words were accepted (the left-hand column) or rejected (the right-hand column) when recorded by at least a third of the speakers:

1: S *bi* for E *be*	2: S *bo* for E *boo* (cf also 23, 24)
4: S *ba* for E *bar*	5: S *bö* for E *burr*
6: S *bäj* for E *bay*	15: S /pUs/ for E *puss*
14: S *puss* for E *puss*	19: S *hem* for E *him*
20: S *örn* for E *earn*	22: S *sinn* for E *seen*

These results agree fairly well with the previous study, although there are som notable differences (cf Johansson 1975a).

In two cases, a S test word was contrasted with two possible E targets. The results indicate clearly that S *hem*, as pronounced by most speakers, is more acceptable as E *hem* than as E *him* (18,

19). Similarly, S sinn, as pronounced by most speakers, is more acceptable as E sin than as E seen (21, 22), though the difference is not as sharp in this case. Finally, the E target puss was contrasted with two possible S test words (14, 15). The results show, for most speakers, a clear difference in favour of S puss.

6.3.2.2 Consonants

In test words where S and E consonants were contrasted there was also a great deal of variation depending upon the speaker. Note, however, that there was complete, or almost complete, acceptance of many test words containing a final (long) consonant preceded by a short vowel (e g 10, 12, 13, 32, 33, 34, 41). This is in agreement with the previous study but could at least partially be attributable to the testing situation. Several test subjects reported after the test that the words were pronounced "very emphatically". Such a pronunciation may very well be objectionable in continuous speech, though it is accepted in a test containing isolated words. It should also be pointed out that an investigation of S and E stops (Johansson 1975a: 87ff) revealed that the acceptability assigned to test words by E listeners decreased as the length of closure of a final stop was systematically extended. The sensitivity to such length variations appeared, however, to be smaller among English than among Swedish listeners.

In several cases, an E target word was contrasted with two possible S equivalents. The S "supradental" [ʈ] and dental /t/ were hardly differentiated in final position due to the unfortunate choice of test word (23, 24); the low acceptability values are certainly due mainly to the vowel (cf 2: bo). In initial position (25, 26), there is some difference in favour of the supradental.[14] It is, however, striking that words containing dental /t/, as pronounced by many speakers, received high acceptability ratings. This is in agreement with the previous study.

The E targets <u>shy</u> and <u>hush</u> were contrasted with test words containing S /ʃ/ or S /ç / (27, 28, 29, 30). Test words containing S /ʃ/ realized as [ʂ] were consistently accepted, whereas those containing S /ʃ/ realized as [ɧ] were completely rejected. The test words beginning or ending in S /ç/ were given high acceptability ratings when pronounced by most speakers, but the acceptance was lower than for [ʂ] among several speakers who realized S /ʃ/ as [ʂ].

Other details which deserve special notice are (1) the comparatively high acceptance of S <u>säll</u> for E <u>sell</u>, as recorded by many speakers (cf the high rating of errors involving the use of clear and dark /l/ in Experiment VI, (2) the low rating of S <u>back</u> for E <u>buck</u> (cf Johansson 1975a: 87ff), (3) the additive effect of subphonemic errors which can be observed most clearly by a comparison of the ratings for S <u>sinn</u>, <u>back</u> vs <u>zink</u> and for S <u>sinn</u>, <u>batt</u> vs <u>sitt</u> (cf Johansson 1975a: 70ff).

In conclusion, it should be noted that very few of the S test words in Experiment VII were completely rejected. The only test words which were rejected completely, regardless of the speaker, due to subphonemic deviations were those containing S /ʃ/ realized as [ɧ] (27, 29) and S /r/ realized as uvular (37). Other cases of complete, or almost complete rejection, involved phonemic deviations, notably S <u>bänn</u> for E <u>ban</u> (11) and S <u>bass</u> for E <u>buzz</u> (42). The deviations are clearly phonemic in these cases, as is shown by the consistent acceptance of S <u>bänn</u> as E <u>Ben</u> (10) and S <u>bass</u> as E <u>bus</u> (13). However, these particular phonemic deviations, i e the substitution of /e/ for /æ/ and /s/ for /z/, were shown in Experiment VI to be less serious than many others. This should be kept in mind in evaluating the degree of gravity of the subphonemic deviations illustrated in Experiment VII.

6.4 Experiment VIII: segmental vs non-segmental errors

So far, nothing has been said about reactions to non-segmental features such as stress and intonation. Experiment VI included one example of incorrect placement of stress (Table 6:1, group 9). Not surprisingly, this received a low rating. Bansal's (1969) investigation of the intelligibility of Indian English showed the importance of prosodic features (cf Section 1.5.1):

> The difference between the more intelligible and the less intelligible Indian speakers of English does not lie in any marked differences in their phonemic system. It is rather in the frequency of mistakes Indian speakers make in the distribution of vowels and consonants and in patterns of word stress, sentence stress, rhythm and intonation. (Bansal 1969: 171).

Bansal's results, based on tests of intelligibility, agree with the rating of foreigners' English pronunciation in Dimitrijević & Djordjević (1971); cf Section 1.51. This study, which was designed to investigate the assessment of pronunciation by different groups of judges, revealed that a group of native speakers of English were comparatively more tolerant in assessing individual sounds than in the assessment of continuous speech. Experiment VIII was designed to investigate if these results would reappear under different conditions.

6.4.1 Material and method

A reading test was prepared consisting of words, sentences and a short text (see Appendix II). The words were selected so as to include examples of all RP vowels and diphthongs as well as consonants which are likely to cause pronunciation problems. The sentences, incidentally identical to the material of Experiment VI, included examples of sounds which are frequently mispronounced by Swedish speakers of English. The text contained examples of all the phonemes of RP but was primarily chosen to test prosodic features.

Reading tests were recorded with beginning university students of English as well as students enrolled in adult education courses in English. The recordings were made in an ordinary classroom using a Tandberg tape-recorder. Before making the recording, the speakers were allowed to read through the text silently and ask questions about unfamiliar words. They were told that the material would be used in a study of the assessment of pronunciation among different groups of judges.

Ten recordings were selected representing different degrees of deviant pronunciation. Seven of the recordings were made by beginning university students (speakers 1, 2, 4, 5, 8, 9, 11 in Table 6:3), three by students enrolled in adult education courses (speakers 6, 10, 12). The former were in their early twenties and had studied English at school for at least seven years; the latter were older and had studied English for 2-4 years. Two additional recordings were added to the ten just mentioned (speakers 3 and 7 in Table 6:3). These were made by experienced pronunciation teachers. Speaker 3 was instructed to read the continuous text without segmental errors but with intonation errors typical of Swedish students of English (especially rises in incorrect places). Speaker 7 was asked to read the text with good intonation but with a number of segmental errors (e g /dʒʌŋ/ for _young_). Both speakers were instructed to make some typical errors in recording the words and sentences in the beginning of the test.

After the recordings had been edited (repeated portions deleted and pauses adjusted), test tapes were prepared containing the twelve recordings in the order specified in Table 6:3. The test tapes were judged by a group of experienced teachers of English as a foreign language. The judges were aged 28-38 and had had at least 6 years' experience of teaching English to foreigners. All were speakers of British English. They were enrolled in an M.A. course in linguistics for language teaching at Lancaster University, England, and were paid to take part in the

Table 6:3 Experiment VIII: results. The figures indicate the mean ratings of words, sentences, and the text assigned by five experienced teachers of English as a foreign language. The speakers are listed in the order in which they appeared on the test tape. The results for speakers 3 and 7 were excluded in calculating the results for the speakers as a group (see the text).

Speaker	Words	Sentences	Text
1	3.87	2.62	2.60
2	3.98	2.88	2.60
(3	3.56	3.18	2.40)
4	3.94	3.20	2.80
5	4.02	3.25	2.20
6	3.80	2.55	1.60
(7	3.73	3.23	3.60)
8	4.07	3.43	3.60
9	3.95	2.77	2.40
10	4.20	2.33	1.80
11	4.18	2.90	3.60
12	3.96	2.82	2.60
All speakers	4.00	2.88	2.58

experiment. Each judge received a test tape, written copies of the test and a test sheet for each speaker (see Appendix III). The following instructions were given:

You will hear twelve foreigners read a series of words, sentences and a short text. Your task is to grade each item on a five-point scale using the test sheets provided:

native-like pronunciation	+ — — — — — −	strong foreign accent

Each speaker should also be given an overall grade using the same scale. If you wish, you may also add comments in the space provided.

The judges worked independently without consulting each other. They spent two to three hours on the task (the test tape lasted approximately 40 minutes).

6.4.2 Experiment VIII: results

As the test was designed to examine the general relationship between segmental and non-segmental errors, reactions to individual words or sentences will not be discussed. Instead, the mean scores for all the words and all the sentences will be compared with those for the continuous text. The scores for "overall impression" will be left out of account, as they hardly differed from the values for the text. Table 6:3 gives the results for each individual speaker as well as for all the speakers combined. The table reveals a consistent difference between the words, on one hand, and the sentences and the text, on the other. For most of the speakers, there is also a difference, in favour of the sentences, between the sentences and the text.

The greater acceptability of the individual words was the result expected. It might be argued that this reflects a high tolerance of mistakes in individual sounds, whereas the lower rating of the sentences and the text is due to a stronger reaction towards non-segmental errors. However, there are problems with this interpretation. First, the individual words normally contained only a single problem point each, whereas there were several in the sentences and the continuous text. Second, it could be argued that it is easier to concentrate on pronouncing one word at a time than to read complete sentences or a text. Hence, we may expect a higher frequency of error in the latter case. The lower rating could then simply have been caused by a higher frequency of error rather than by a difference of error type. Finally, the mixture of errors which are easily acceptable individually might give an incongruous effect in continuous speech and lead to a decline in acceptability.

In spite of these problems of interpretation, there are definite reasons to attribute the low rating of, especially, the text to non-segmental errors. Note the low rating of the text as recorded by speaker 3, who avoided segmental errors consistently, and the high rating of the text when recorded by speaker 7, whose recording included segmental errors (cf the preceding section). The reason for this clear contrast must be that speaker 3 was instructed to read the text with deviant prosody, whereas speaker 7 was asked to use good intonation. This is also suggested by judges' comments:

Speaker 3: "Quite good pronunciation of the text but the effect was spoiled by intonation." - "This student tends to use the rising tone at any utterance final point. He seems also to be unsure about stress - not just wrong - unsure."

Speaker 7: "Very good intonation." - "This student... has a go and his text is the best yet in terms of conveying a grasp of the stress and tonic system of English."

Judges' comments were rather few. The comments which did occur, however, almost all drew attention to the deviant prosody of many recordings.[15]

The conclusion to be drawn from Experiment VIII seems then to be that non-segmental errors cause a greater degree of deviance than segmental ones. This finding agrees with the results from Bansal (1969) and Dimitrijević & Djordjević (1971) mentioned in Section 6.4.[16] The greater severity of prosodic as opposed to segmental deviance can also be argued on more general grounds. Nash (1972: 570ff) points out that phonemic interference can be resolved by context, whereas this is not possible with prosodic interference: "the listener cannot use linguistic context to help him, because preceding utterances also have inappropriate and unresolved prosodic patterns and the listener is unable to relate the total meaning of one utterance to the total meaning of the next." In spite of all the evidence showing the greater relative importance of correct prosody, there must certainly be a minimum of segmental correctness to ensure intelligibility. What Experiment VIII shows is that, with some typical Swedish speakers of English (whose accent may not be very deviant in an absolute sense; cf note 15), prosodic errors are more striking than errors in the pronunciation of individual sounds.

6.5 Summary and applications

The studies reported in this chapter have attempted to rank the gravity of different types of phonological errors. Segmental errors were found to cause a lower degree of deviance than errors in prosody. There was a great deal of variation between individual segmental errors, phonemic as well as subphonemic. Though there was a tendency for the former to be judged as more serious than the latter, this was not always the case. Other findings were that the direction of substitution was important in phonemic errors and that consonant errors were often judged as more serious than vowel errors. There are many points of detail which deserve further investigation, especially reactions to specific types of segmental and non-segmental deviance. It would also be of interest to repeat some of the experiments with different speakers or groups of judges. Note, finally, that the present experiments were more or less artificial, as they were designed to investigate particular problems and eliminate irrelevant factors (such as variations in meaning and context). It would certainly be important to examine if the same results appear in more natural language situations.

The results reported should not be taken to mean that certain areas of phonology could be left out of account entirely in teaching English to Swedes. They rather indicate the emphasis that should be given to specific features in teaching. They also have natural applications in testing, as they provide better criteria for assessment than have been available so far.

A ranking of various aspects of pronunciation according to native speakers' reactions enables us to take up a position between the extreme views (cf Lado 1961: 39) that either deny the importance of pronunciation altogether (which might endanger communication) or assume that nothing short of nativeness is adequate (which is an unattainable goal for most learners). By adopting the middle position we can both secure the success of communication and enjoy the advantages which a foreign accent may provide and which Haugen (as quoted by Diller, 1971: 99) has formulated by saying that "a foreign accent is a person's best passport".[17]

NOTES

1 I am grateful to fil kand Stig Olsson for recording the material used in the experiment.

2 The distribution was as follows: Cheshire (1), Durham (1), Essex (1), Gloucestershire (1), Hampshire (1), Hertfordshire (2), Lancashire (2), Middlesex (1), Norfolk (1), Northern Ireland (1), Surrey (1), Wales (2), Wiltshire (1), Yorkshire (2). Four subjects had lived in a variety of places within the United Kingdom. One subject gave no information on place of residence.

3 See e g Stubelius (1968: 11ff). This view is also implicit in Lado's (1961: 40) arguments for a phonemic criterion of accuracy in pronunciation testing. Cf further Halliday et al (1964: 84), "Transference of phonetic habits... is easier to tolerate and harder to avoid than transference at other levels"; Mackey (1970: 201), "... when getting the hang of a foreign accent, the strange sound which consistently replaces a certain allophone in the stream of speech does not on each occurrence add much new information to the message. We come to expect it and take it for granted, for it can be predicted. In other words, the more predictable the interference, the less it interferes." For another view on the relationship between phonemic and subphonemic errors, see note 4.

4 Our results should be compared with those of Prator (1957: XIIff), who reports a frequency count of the pronunciation difficulties of a large number of foreign learners of English and asks the question whether there were "certain kinds of difficulty which were more serious than others, which affected intelligibility to a greater extent, and which consequently must be given greater emphasis". Prator refuses to accept the widely believed view that errors involving the substitution of one phoneme for another are more serious than nonphonemic errors and states that "certain nonphonemic 'errors' proved in practice to be serious barriers to intelligibility."

5 Cf e g Weinreich, Labov & Herzog (1968: 130ff).

6 The recording took place in an echo-free room on a Studer A62 tape-recorder using a Sennheiser MD421 microphone. The recording speed was 7.5 i.p.s.

7 In making the recording the speakers used a list of the test words in orthographic form (apart from test items 15 and 26, which were represented as in Table 6:2). The lists were practised before the recording was begun to make sure that the speakers knew what "phonemes" to use. None of the speakers knew the object of the test before making the recording.

8 The distribution was as follows. Group A: Berkshire (1), Buckinghamshire (1), Devon (1), Durham (1), Essex (1), Hampshire (1), Lancashire (4), Middlesex (1), Norfolk (1), Staffordshire (1), Surrey (1), Wales (1), Warwickshire (1), Wiltshire (1), Yorkshire (2). Group 2: Cheshire (2), Durham (1), Gloucestershire (1), Hertfordshire (2), Lancashire (1), London (3), Norfolk (1), Northern Ireland (1), Nottinghamshire (1), Surrey (1), Wales (1), Yorkshire (2). Three subjects in group A had lived in a variety of places within the United Kingdom. One subject in group A and two in group B gave no information on place of residence.

9 Some of the speakers realized /ɛ/ in *hem* as [e].

10 /ʃ/ in *sjaj* was realized as [ʂ] by some speakers (2, 3, 5, 8, 9, 10, 12), as [ɧ] by the rest.

11 /ʃ/ in *hasch* was realized as [ʂ] by some speakers (2, 3, 5, 8, 9, 10, 12, 16), as [ɧ] by the rest.

12 /r/ in *rann* was realized as [R] or [ʁ] by some speakers (1, 4, 6, 7, 14, 15), as [r], or sometimes [ɹ] by the rest.

13 "Acceptance" and "rejection" in this context (and the rest of the section) are defined with reference to the + and - scores in Table 6:2.

14 Before making the recording, the speakers practised the pronunciation of [ʈ] in initial position by saying [bu:ʈ] and [ʈaj] several times in immediate succession. Nevertheless, some speakers had difficulties in making the recording. The results should therefore be regarded with some caution.

15 One judge made general comments on the test. Note especially: "As none of the speakers have strong foreign accents in a subjective sense, I have used the 5-point scale as if it were designed to point out relative differences between the speakers. Otherwise almost all speakers would fall into the 2 group and no differentiation would be possible."

16 Cf also Svensson (1974: 102), "If it is true that prosody is an important link in the perceptual process, then we must devote more energy and time to the teaching of prosodic patterns, and relatively less time to the teaching of the pronunciation of single sounds and words. Some support for this view can be found in the observation that a foreigner can make many errors without being unintelligible, as long as his production of prosodic patterns is fairly correct."

17 Cf further Diller, *loc cit*, "... it [the foreign accent] warns the listener not to be surprised if he finds other mistakes. And if there are no other mistakes, people will notice how well the foreigner speaks their language."

APPENDIX I. SWEDISH WORD LISTS: SPEAKERS

Number	Sex	Age	Place of residence
1	M	20	Småland
2	M	21	Stockholm
3	F	25	Göteborg
4	M	31	Halland
5	F	19	Bohuslän
6	M	30	Malmö
7	F	20	Simrishamn
8	M	21	Stockholm
9	M	35	Vänersborg
10	F	38	Kungälv
11	F	19	Dalarna
12	M	26	Västmanland
13	M	35	Stockholm
14	M	36	Småland
15	F	19	Småland
16	F	40	Stockholm

Note:

The place of residence indicates the place or area where the speaker spent most of his or her life (at least the years 1-12).

APPENDIX II: THE READING TEST

A Words:

be
boo
bore
bar
burr
bay
by
boy
bin
Ben
ban
bun
puss
boss
beer
bear
boor
bow (for shooting arrows)
bow (to bend the head)
fire
tie
shy
rye
try
but
buck
sell
yes
ladies
quite
wife
cheap
joke
pleasure
boys
human
exam
butter
bath
father

B Sentences:

There was an explosion near the station.
They visited Land's End.
Let's sing something else.
There was ice on the road.
Mr Wilson is a writer.
Some people don't like milk.
This boat is very cheap.
This is Miss Jones.
Ted is interested in politics.
John is a young architect.
Sarah sings very well.
They don't want to do it.

C Text:

One day last week, I took a train to Chester. I saw with pleasure that there were only two people in my compartment - myself and another young man. I thought he looked rather thin and shy. During the whole journey, he was busy staring at me. After about four hours, he suddenly spoke to me. "Do you belive in ghosts?" he said. "Of course not", I replied. "Surely *you* don't?" He smiled very slowly, nodded his head, and in a sad little voice, he answered, "Yes, I do", and disappeared.

APPENDIX III: TEST SHEET

____
(number of speaker)

	Word				Word			
A	be	+	_ _ _ _ _	-	tie	+	_ _ _ _ _	-
	boo	+	_ _ _ _ _	-	shy	+	_ _ _ _ _	-
	bore	+	_ _ _ _ _	-	rye	+	_ _ _ _ _	-
	bar	+	_ _ _ _ _	-	try	+	_ _ _ _ _	-
	burr	+	_ _ _ _ _	-	but	+	_ _ _ _ _	-
	bay	+	_ _ _ _ _	-	buck	+	_ _ _ _ _	-
	by	+	_ _ _ _ _	-	sell	+	_ _ _ _ _	-
	boy	+	_ _ _ _ _	-	yes	+	_ _ _ _ _	-
	bin	+	_ _ _ _ _	-	ladies	+	_ _ _ _ _	-
	Ben	+	_ _ _ _ _	-	quite	+	_ _ _ _ _	-
	ban	+	_ _ _ _ _	-	wife	+	_ _ _ _ _	-
	bun	+	_ _ _ _ _	-	cheap	+	_ _ _ _ _	-
	puss	+	_ _ _ _ _	-	joke	+	_ _ _ _ _	-
	boss	+	_ _ _ _ _	-	pleasure	+	_ _ _ _ _	-
	beer	+	_ _ _ _ _	-	boys	+	_ _ _ _ _	-
	bear	+	_ _ _ _ _	-	human	+	_ _ _ _ _	-
	boor	+	_ _ _ _ _	-	exam	+	_ _ _ _ _	-
	bow (a curve)	+	_ _ _ _ _	-	butter	+	_ _ _ _ _	-
	bow (to bow)	+	_ _ _ _ _	-	bath	+	_ _ _ _ _	-
	fire	+	_ _ _ _ _	-	father	+	_ _ _ _ _	-

B
- There was an explosion near the station. + _ _ _ _ _ -
- They visited Land's End. + _ _ _ _ _ -
- Let's sing something else. + _ _ _ _ _ -
- There was ice on the road. + _ _ _ _ _ -
- Mr Wilson is a writer. + _ _ _ _ _ -
- Some people don't like milk. + _ _ _ _ _ -
- This boat is very cheap. + _ _ _ _ _ -
- This is Miss Jones. + _ _ _ _ _ -
- Ted is interested in politics. + _ _ _ _ _ -
- John is a young architect. + _ _ _ _ _ -
- Sarah sings very well. + _ _ _ _ _ -
- They don't want to do it. + _ _ _ _ _ -

C The text + _ _ _ _ _ -

OVERALL IMPRESSION + _ _ _ _ _ -

COMMENTS:

7 Native vs Non-native Judges

7.1 Background

It has sometimes been stated that native speakers are more tolerant towards learners' errors than are foreign speakers, especially language teachers, with the same native-language background as the learners. Nickel (1972: 19f), who makes an observation of this kind, attributes the greater tolerance of the native partly to a positive attitude in general towards foreigners learning his language, partly to the native's greater knowledge of his language and its varieties. The discrepancy between judgements of natives and non-natives is well illustrated by the results of Experiments III and IV, where groups of natives rated texts containing specific types of errors which had previously been marked by a committee of Swedish teachers of English (cf Chapter 4; note the marks quoted in the Appendix). However, in this case the two groups of judges were faced with partially different tasks, which might account for the discrepancy of judgement. To provide a safer basis of comparison, part of the material of Experiments II and VII was submitted to non-native as well as native judges. Here the two groups of judges were given exactly the same tasks and received the same instructions.

7.2 Experiment II: native vs non-native judges

Ten of the papers used in Experiment II (cf Section 3.2) were selected and presented to two groups of Swedish teachers of English or prospective teachers of English who were enrolled in a teacher-training course (G1, G2).[1] G1 received four papers in their original form and four in corrected versions; G2 received the opposite versions of the same papers. Common to G1 and G2 were two papers which only appeared in their original

Table 7:1 Experiment II: mean ratings of texts in original (O) and corrected (C) versions. Test subjects: 24 non-native judges (G1: 9, G2: 15). A higher figure indicates a higher rating on the five-point scale (+5...1-). For comparison, the ratings of the native judges are given within parentheses (cf Chapter 3, Table 3:1).

Paper	G1	G2
1	C: 4.33 (3.55)	O: 2.93 (2.33)
3	O: 3.17 (2.82)	C: 3.87 (4.08)
5	O: 3.00 (3.27)	O: 2.80 (3.58)
9	O: 4.00 (2.82)	O: 3.33 (3.58)
10	C: 4.33 (3.91)	O: 2.80 (2.42)
14	C: 4.00 (4.27)	O: 3.27 (3.00)
15	C: 3.17 (4.09)	O: 2.93 (2.92)
16	O: 2.33 (2.82)	C: 3.07 (4.08)
18	O: 2.47 (2.09)	C: 2.93 (4.08)
19	O: 2.17 (2.09)	C: 3.13 (3.42)

Table 7:2 Experiment II: mean ratings of original and corrected versions of papers judged by the non-native subjects. For comparison, the ratings of the native judges are given within parentheses.

Papers	Version		
	Corr	Orig	
1, 10, 14, 15 (a)	G1: 3.96 (3.96)	G2: 2.98 (2.67)	M_a: 3.47 (3.32)
3, 16, 18, 19 (b)	G2: 3.25 (3.92)	G1: 2.54 (2.46)	M_b: 2.90 (3.19)
	M_{Corr}: 3.61 (3.94)	M_{Orig}: 2.76 (2.57)	

form. Both groups received instructions A, i e they were asked to grade the papers on a five-point scale ranging from "very good" to "very bad". Through an error in administration, more subjects were assigned to G2 (N: 15) than to G1 (N: 9).

The results, which are given in Table 7:1, show the same tendencies as those of the native judges. The corrected versions have received consistently higher ratings than the papers in their original form. The differences between the ratings of correct and incorrect papers are shown more clearly in Table 7:2. It is interesting to note that the non-native judges have actually been less influenced by the errors than were the natives. However, this is partially due to the somewhat narrower dispersion of the mean ratings in the former group.[2] In any case, it seems safe to say that the results do not support the idea of a greater tolerance of overt errors among native than among non-native judges.

7.3 Experiment VIII: native vs non-native judges

Four of the speakers in Experiment VIII (Cf Section 6.4) were selected and their recordings were played to a group of 10 Swedish teachers of English. These received exactly the same instructions as the native judges, i e they were asked to grade a series of words, sentences, and a short text recorded by each speaker on a five-point scale ranging from "native-like pronunciation" to "strong foreign accent". The whole group listened to the test tape at the same time and only once, whereas the native judges worked individually and were able to spend as much time as they wanted listening to the recordings. The ratings were recorded separately by each judge on a test sheet prepared for each speaker (cf Chapter 3, Appendix III).

The results are given in Table 7:3. The table reveals a consistent difference between the native and the non-native judges. The individual words were judged far more severely by the latter

Table 7:3 Experiment VIII: mean ratings of words, sentences, and text assigned by 10 non-native judges. A higher figure indicates a higher rating on the five-point scale (+5...1-). The speakers are listed in the order in which they appeared on the test tape. The ratings of the native judges are given within parentheses (cf Chapter 6, Table 6:3).

Speaker	Words	Sentences	Text
2	3.32 (3.98)	3.08 (2.88)	3.10 (2.60)
3	2.50 (3.56)	2.73 (3.18)	2.90 (2.40)
7	2.86 (3.73)	2.98 (3.23)	3.90 (3.60)
1	3.44 (3.87)	2.62 (2.62)	2.50 (2.60)
Mean	3.03 (3.79)	2.85 (2.98)	3.10 (2.80)

group. On the other hand, there is a tendency among the natives to judge the text more severely. These reactions could be interpreted as differences in the relative importance of segmental and prosodic interference. The results agree very well with those of Dimitrijević & Djordjević (1971), who compared the assessment of Yugoslav university students' English pronunciation by native as well as non-native judges (cf Section 1.5.1). We seem to be able to conclude that natives are more tolerant in the assessment of individual sounds than non-natives but less so in the assessment of prosody.

7.4 Conclusion

The two experiments are obviously insufficient to solve the problem of possible differences between native and non-native judges in the rating of overt errors.[3] They do indicate, however, that there may be differences as regards the relative importance of different error types rather than a greater general tolerance of errors among native judges. The practical conclusion to be drawn from Experiment VIII is that non-native teachers of English should change their priorities in the area of pronunciation and attach more importance to prosody.

NOTES

1 I am grateful to Moira Linnarud, Department of English, Lund, and Torsten Lindblad, Department of Educational Research, Gothenburg School of Education, for their assistance in administering the tests.

2 The mean and standard deviation for the 20 mean ratings were 3.20 and .62 for the non-native judges. The corresponding figures for the native judges were 3.26 and .71.

3 Ideally, the study should have compared the reactions of non-native judges with those of different groups of native evaluators, especially trained evaluators and native speakers without any kind of teacher training (cf Gorosch 1973).

8 Summary, Applications, and Suggestions for Further Research

8.1 Summary

The following chapter-by-chapter survey briefly summarizes the results of the investigation. The figures within parentheses refer to section numbers.

Chapter 1 defines the area of error evaluation (1.1), outlines a programme of research (1.4), and surveys previous work in error gravity and related areas (1.5). Error evaluation is a complement to error analysis and is concerned with establishing error gravity. The principles of comprehensibility and degree of irritation define a hierarchy of errors, together with the principles of generality and frequency (1.3). Research is needed to study the comprehensibility and degree of irritation of different error types, as evidenced by receiver reactions. It is also necessary to examine how the reactions might vary depending upon characteristics of the receiver, the type of language situation, and the role of the sender.

Chapter 2 is concerned with methodology and examines the relationship between subjective and objective measures of error gravity. Subjective measures are judgements of error gravity made by test subjects; objective measures are those obtained from performance tests where subjects are unaware that the object is to establish a hierarchy of errors (2.1). A previous experiment is described which showed good agreement between the two methods (2.2). A new analogous experiment (Experiment I, 2.3) gave a similar result. It is concluded that the rest of the investigation can be based mainly on the simpler judgement technique.

Chapter 3 attempts to evaluate the importance of overt errors in native speakers' judgements of the quality of written material produced by foreigners. In an experiment (Experiment II, 3.2) native speakers were asked to judge short papers in their original form and in corrected versions according to two sets of instructions. Results showed that the judges were affected by the overt errors both in rating the papers on a scale from "very good" to "very bad" and, though less so, in judging "how successfully the writer has handled the topic". This means that the results of a partially analogous experiment by Landén & Trankell (1975) cannot be generalized and taken as evidence that overt errors are unimportant under all circumstances.

Chapter 4 gives an account of two experiments (Experiment III, 4.2; Experiment IV, 4.3) where native speakers were asked to interpret or rank passages containing specific types of lexical and grammatical errors produced by Swedish learners of English. The experiments showed that the native speakers had greater problems in interpreting lexical than grammatical errors and also judged the former to be more severe than the latter. It is suggested that the principle of generality, which assigns a higher degree of gravity to grammatical than to lexical errors, may often have been given too much weight at the expense of the communicative principle.

Chapter 5 studies the relationship between foreign accent and speech distortion in an experiment (Experiment V, 5.2) where groups of Swedish and English school children listened to English texts read by Swedes and native speakers of English. The results were more or less the same for the Swedish school children when they listened to natives or foreigners. For the English school children there was a gap between understanding the native and the foreigner, and this grew wider under conditions of distortion. The result demonstrates the need to eliminate features of foreign accent, even though they may seem unimportant under optimal circumstances.

In Chapter 6 an attempt is made to rank different types of phonological errors typical of Swedish learners of English. Different types of segmental errors are studied in Experiment VI

(6.2) where native speakers judged a series of sentences pronounced erroneously in two or more ways. The degree of severity was found to vary considerably both for phonemic and subphonemic errors. Though there was a tendency for the former to be judged as more severe than the latter, this was not always the case. Other findings were that consonant errors tended to be judged as more serious than vowel errors and that the direction of substitution was important in phonemic errors. Experiment VII (6.3) studies the degree of deviance of subphonemic errors in English due to substitution from Swedish by asking native speakers to rate the acceptability of Swedish material (words or nonsense words) as representations of similar-sounding English words. The results revealed interesting details concerning the relationship between Swedish and English sounds but showed considerable variability depending upon the Swedish speaker. Experiment VIII (6.4) consisted of recordings of English words, sentences, and a short text by Swedish learners of English. Each item was judged on a five-point scale by a group of native speakers. These gave consistently higher ratings to the words than to the sentences and the text, which is taken to indicate that native speakers attach more importance to errors in prosody than to errors in individual sounds.

Chapter 7 compares reactions of native and non-native (Swedish) judges in two of the experiments reported in earlier chapters. Part of the material of Experiment II was submitted to a group of Swedish teachers of English or prospective teachers of English (7.2). The results were similar to those obtained with the native judges. Another group of Swedish teachers of English was asked to judge part of the material of Experiment VIII (7.3). The result showed a consistent difference with respect to the native judges, who gave higher ratings to the individual words than did the non-natives and tended to give lower ratings to the text. This is taken to indicate that natives are more tolerant in the assessment of individual sounds than non-natives but less so in the assessment of prosody. The results of the two experiments do not support the alleged greater tolerance of overt errors among native speakers.

8.2 A note on applications

When it is discovered that linguistic deviance meets with negative reactions, a possible remedy is to work for greater tolerance among receivers (cf the quotations given at the beginning of the investigation, p ii). This is a possibility which should not be overlooked, though it would seem to apply more to varying uses acquired among natives than to errors among foreign learners. The attitude taken up here is that the study of error gravity may help indicate areas which should be given priority in teaching and testing a foreign language (cf Chapter 1, Fig 1:1). Needless to say, it is only one of the factors to be taken into account, and its importance should not be exaggerated. The study of error gravity must not lead to over-emphasis of certain areas at the expense of teaching the foreign language as a complete system of communication.

8.3 Suggestions for further research

The present investigation does not exhaust the research programme outlined in Section 1.4. Such factors as differing reactions depending upon the type of receiver, the type of language situation, and, especially, foreigner role, need further investigation. Even the investigation of error type is incomplete. In particular, further studies must examine "mistakes" in the sense of Corder (1973: 259), i e failures to match the language to the situation or inappropriate rather than unacceptable uses of language.[1] Here we must note Corder's (1973: 261, 281f) observation that we assign a special role to the foreigner in which behaviour, inappropriate as a native, is socially acceptable but which may also mean that certain uses of language are inappropriate for the foreigner, though current among native speakers.

In conclusion, the study must not be limited to cases of overt deviance but must also establish their importance as compared with covert errors. As pointed out in Section 1.4, we must then widen the question and ask how variations in learner language in general affect communication. Such a study could be carried out by correlating native-speaker judgements with particular aspects, positive as well as negative, of material produced by foreign learners (cf Section 2.1).

NOTES

1 For an observation on the frequency of such errors, cf Halliday et al (1964: 88), "The choice of items from the wrong register, and the mixing of items from different registers, are among the most frequent mistakes made by non-native speakers of a language". Note also an observation by Labov (1970: 64f) on the interpretation of this type of deviance among natives speaking different dialects, "Though native speakers of a given dialect show an extraordinary ability to interpret the grammatical rules of another dialect, they do not necessarily show the same ability in dealing with the broader aspects of communicative competence. The rules of discourse tend to differ not in obligatory sequencing rules, but in the interpretation of the social significance of actions - differences in the forms of politeness, ways of mitigating or expressing anger, or of displaying sincerity and trust. This is an area where ethnographic and linguistic description has an important role to play."

Bibliography

Aborn, M, Rubenstein, H and Sterling, T D, 1959, "Sources of Contextual Constraint Upon Words in Sentences", *Journal of Experimental Psychology* 57, 171-80.

Abrams, K and Bever, T G, 1969, "Syntactic Structure Modifies Attention During Speech Perception and Recognition", *Quarterly Journal of Experimental Psychology* 21, 280-90.

Ahlgren, I, 1975, *Interaction Between Form and Content in Speech Perception*, Stockholm: Institute of Linguistics.

Anisfeld, M, 1974, "Social Perception of Speech", in T A Sebeok, ed, *Current Trends in Linguistics*, Vol 12, The Hague: Mouton, 1429-42.

Bailey, B L, 1971, "Jamaican Creole: Can Dialect Boundaries Be Defined?" In D Hymes, ed, *Pidginization and Creolization of Languages*, Cambridge University Press, 341-48.

Bansal, R K, 1965/66, *The Intelligibility of Indian English: Measurements of the Intelligibility of Connected Speech and Sentence and Word Material, Presented to Listeners of Different Nationalities*, Ph D dissertation, University College, London.

Bansal, R K, 1969, *The Intelligibility of Indian English*, Monograph No 4, Central Institute of English, Hyderabad, India.

Black, J W and Singh, S, 1968, "The Psychological Basis of Phonetics", in B Malmberg, ed, *Manual of Phonetics*, Amsterdam: North-Holland Publishing Company, 105-128.

Bloomfield, L, 1944, "Secondary and Tertiary Responses to Language", *Language* 20, 45-55.

Bradley, M, 1970, "Effects on Reading Tests of Deletions of Selected Grammatical Categories", *Nineteenth Yearbook of the National Reading Conference*, Milwaukee, Wisc, 87-93.

Brennan, E M, Ryan, E B and Dawson, W E, 1975, "Scaling of Apparent Accentedness by Magnitude Estimation and Sensory Modality Matching", *Journal of Psycholinguistic Research* 4, 27-36.

Brodkey, D, 1972, "Dictation as a Measure of Mutual Intelligibility", *Language Learning* 22, 203-20.

Bruce, D J, 1956, "Effects of Context Upon Intelligibility of Heard Speech", in C Cherry, ed, *Information Theory*, London: Butterworth, 245-52.

Burgschmidt, E and Götz, D, 1974, *Kontrastive Linguistik Deutsch/Englisch: Theorie und Anwendung*, München: Max Hueber Verlag.

Buros, A K, ed, 1965, *The Sixth Mental Measurements Yearbook*, Highland Park, N J: Gryphon.

Burt, M and Kiparsky, C, 1972, The Gooficon, Rowley, Mass: Newbury House.

Chaiklin, J B, 1955, "Native American Listeners' Adaptation in Understanding Speakers with Foreign Dialect", Journal of Speech and Hearing Disorders 20, 165-70.

Cherry, C, 1966, On Human Communication, 2nd ed, Cambridge, Mass: M I T Press.

Chomsky, N, 1961, "Some Methodological Remarks on Generative Grammar", Word 17, 219-39.

Chomsky, N, 1965, Aspects of the Theory of Syntax, Cambridge, Mass: M I T Press.

Chreist, F M, 1964, Foreign Accent, Englewood Cliffs, N J: Prentice-Hall.

Coleman, E B, 1965, "Responses to a Scale of Grammaticalness", Journal of Verbal Learning and Verbal Behavior 4, 521-27.

Cooper, R L and Fishman, J A, 1974, "The Study of Language Attitudes", Linguistics 136, 5-19.

Corder, S P, 1973, Introducing Applied Linguistics, Harmondsworth: Penguin Books.

Corder, S P, 1975, "Error Analysis, Interlanguage and Second Language Acquisition", Language Teaching & Linguistics: Abstracts 8, 201-18.

Danks, J H, 1969, "Grammaticalness and Meaningfulness in the Comprehension of Sentences", Journal of Verbal Learning and Verbal Behavior 8, 687-96.

Danks, J H and Glucksberg, S, 1970, "Psychological Scaling of Linguistic Properties", Language and Speech 13, 118-38.

Davy, D and Quirk, R, 1969, "An Acceptability Experiment with Spoken Output", Journal of Linguistics 5, 109-20.

Diller, K, 1971, Generative Grammar, Structural Linguistics, and Language Teaching, Rowley, Mass: Newbury House.

Dimitrijević, N R and Djordjević, D, 1971, "The Reliability of the Subjective Assessment of the Pupils' Pronunciation of English as a Foreign Language", International Review of Applied Linguistics 9, 245-65.

Downey, R G and Hakes, D T, 1968, "Some Psychological Effects of Violating Linguistic Rules", Journal of Verbal Learning and Verbal Behavior 7, 158-61.

Engh, B, 1971, "En toleransundersökning: tyska elever tolkar svenska elevers språkfel", Pedagogisk-psykologiska problem, No 137, Lärarhögskolan, Malmö.

Enkvist, N E, 1973, "Should We Count Errors or Measure Success?" In J Svartvik, ed, Errata, Lund: C W K Gleerup, 16-23.

Fillenbaum, S, 1970, "On the Use of Memorial Techniques to Assess Syntactic Structures", Psychological Bulletin 73, 231-37.

Fillenbaum, S and Jones, L V, 1962, "An Application of 'Cloze' Technique to the Study of Aphasic Speech", Journal of Abnormal and Social Psychology 65, 183-89.

Fillenbaum, S, Jones, L V and Rapoport, A, 1963, "The Predictability of Words and Their Grammatical Classes as a Function of Rate of Deletion from a Speech Transcript", Journal of Verbal Learning and Verbal Behavior 2, 186-94.

Fillmore, Ch J, 1972, "On Generativity", in S Peters, ed, Goals of Linguistic Theory, Englewood Cliffs, N J: Prentice-Hall, 1-19.

Foss, D J, 1969, "Decision Processes During Sentence Comprehension: Effects of Lexical Item Difficulty and Position Upon Decision Times", Journal of Verbal Learning and Verbal Behavior 8, 457-62.

Foss, D and Lynch, R H, 1969, "Decision Processes During Sentence Comprehension: Effects of Surface Structure on Decision Times", Perception and Psychophysics 5, 145-48.

Giles, H, 1970, "Evaluative Reactions to Accents", Educational Review 22, 211-27.

Gimson, A C, 1970, An Introduction to the Pronunciation of English, 2nd ed, London: Arnold.

Gladney, T A and Krulee, G K, 1967, "The Influence of Syntactic Errors on Sentence Recognition", Journal of Verbal Learning and Verbal Behavior 6, 692-98.

Gorosch, M, 1973, "Assessment Intervariability in Testing Oral Performance of Adult Students", in J Svartvik, ed, Errata, Lund: C W K Gleerup, 145-52.

Halliday, M A K, McIntosh, A and Strevens, P D, 1964, The Linguistic Sciences and Language Teaching, London: Longman.

Haugen, E, 1975, "The Curse of Babel", in E Haugen and M Bloomfield, eds, Language as a Human Problem, Guildford & London: Lutterworth Press, 33-43.

Healy, A F and Miller, G A, 1971, "The Relative Contribution of Nouns and Verbs to Sentence Acceptability and Comprehensibility", Psychonomic Science 24, 94-96.

Hersvall, M, Lindell, E and Pettersson, I L, 1974, "Om kvalitet i gymnasisters skriftspråk: rapport från projektet 'Svenska mått'", Pedagogisk-psykologiska problem, No 253, Pedagogisk-psykologiska institutionen, Lärarhögskolan, Malmö.

Hill, A A, 1961, "Grammaticality", Word 17, 1-10.

Hoenigswald, H M, 1966, "A Proposal for the Study of Folk Linguistics", in W Bright, ed, Sociolinguistics, The Hague: Mouton, 16-26.

Hymes, D H, 1972, "On Communicative Competence", in J B Pride and J Holmes, eds, Sociolinguistics, Harmondsworth: Penguin Books, 269-93.

James, C, 1972, "The Diagnosis and Analysis of Error - Some Insights from Linguistics", Audio-Visual Language Journal 10, 75-79.

James, C, 1974, "Linguistic Measures for Error Gravity", Audio-Visual Language Journal 12, 3-9.

Johansson, S, 1975a, Papers in Contrastive Linguistics and Language Testing, Lund: C W K Gleerup.

Johansson, S, 1975b, "Problems in Studying the Communicative Effect of Learners' Errors", Colloque 'Theoretical Models in Applied Linguistics' IV, Université de Neuchâtel, 29-31 May, 1975.

Jordan, E P, 1960, "Articulation Test Measures and Listener Ratings of Articulation Defectiveness", Journal of Speech and Hearing Research 3, 303-319.

Juhász, J, 1970, Probleme der Interferenz, München: Max Hueber Verlag.

Kainz, F, 1959, "Psychologie der Sprache", in R Luchsinger and G E Arnold, Lehrbuch der Stimm- und Sprachheilkunde, 2nd ed, Wien: Springer.

Katz, J J, 1964, "Semi-Sentences", in J A Fodor and J J Katz, eds, The Structure of Language, Englewood Cliffs, N J: Prentice-Hall, 400-416.

Kirk, P L, 1970, "Dialect Intelligibility Testing: The Mazatec Study", International Journal of American Linguistics 36, 205-11.

Kolers, P A, 1968, "Reading Temporally and Spatially Transformed Text", in K S Goodman, ed, The Psycholinguistic Nature of the Reading Process, Detroit: Wayne State University Press, 27-40.

Kolers, P A, 1969, "Reading Is Only Incidentally Visual", in K S Goodman and J T Fleming, eds, Psycholinguistics and the Teaching of Reading, Newark, Del: International Reading Association, 8-16.

Krulee, G K and Ramsburg, R E, 1974, "Semantic Anomalies and Sentence Recognition", Perceptual and Motor Skills 38, 1275-86.

Labov, W, 1966, The Social Stratification of English in New York City, Washington, D C: Center for Applied Linguistics.

Labov, W, 1970, "The Place of Linguistic Research in American Society", in Linguistics in the 1970's, Washington, D C: Center for Applied Linguistics.

Lado, R, 1961, Language Testing, London: Longman.

Lambert, W E, Hodgson, R C, Gardner, R C and Fillenbaum, S, 1960, "Evaluational Reactions to Spoken Languages", Journal of Abnormal and Social Psychology 60, 44-51.

Landén, R and Trankell, A, 1975, "Människor som talar svenska med brytning", in Invandrarproblem: Fem uppsatser om invandrar- och minoritetsproblem från IMFO-gruppen vid Stockholms Universitet, Stockholm: Pan/Norstedts, 23-71.

Lane, H, 1963, "Foreign Accent and Speech Distortion", Journal of the Acoustic Society of America 35, 451-53.

Lazerson, B H, 1974/75, "The Influence of Highly Variable Spelling Upon the Reading Performance of Skilled Readers of Modern English", Reading Research Quarterly 10, 583-615.

Lee, R R, 1971, "Dialect Perception: A Critical Review and Re-Evaluation", Quarterly Journal of Speech 57, 410-17.

Leisi, E, 1972, "Theoretische Grundlagen der Fehlerbewertung", in G Nickel, ed, Fehlerkunde, Berlin: Cornelsen-Velhagen & Klasing, 25-37.

Levelt, W J M, 1974, Formal Grammars in Linguistics and Psycholinguistics, III: Psycholinguistic Applications, The Hague: Mouton.

Levelt, W J M, 1975, "Skill Theory and Language Teaching", Colloque 'Theoretical Models in Applied Linguistics' IV, Université de Neuchâtel, 29-31 May, 1975.

Licklider, J C R and Miller, G A, 1951, "The Perception of Speech", in S S Stevens, ed, Handbook of Experimental Psychology, New York: Wiley, 1040-74.

Linnarud, M, 1975,"Lexis in Free Production. An Analysis of the Lexical Texture of Swedish Students' Written Work", Swedish-English Contrastive Studies, No 6, Department of English, Lund University.

Louthan, V, 1965, "Some Systematic Grammatical Deletions and Their Effects on Reading Comprehension", English Journal 54, 295-99.

Mackey, W F, 1970, "Interference, Integration and the Synchronic Fallacy", in J E Alatis, ed, Report of the Twenty-First Annual Round Table Meeting on Linguistics and Language Studies, Washington, D C: Georgetown University Press, 195-227.

Maclay, H and Sleator, M D, 1960, "Responses to Language: Judgements of Grammaticalness", International Journal of American Linguistics 26, 275-282.

Marks, L E, 1967, "Judgements of Grammaticalness of Some English Sentences and Semi-Sentences", American Journal of Psychology 80, 196-204.

Marks, L E, 1968, "Scaling of Grammaticalness of Self-Embedded English Sentences", Journal of Verbal Learning and Verbal Behavior 7, 965-67.

Marks, L E and Miller, G A, 1964, "The Role of Semantic and Syntactic Constraints in the Memorization of English Sentences", Journal of Verbal Learning and Verbal Behavior 3, 1-5.

Meyer-Eppler, W, 1959, Grundlagen und Anwendungen der Informationstheorie, Berlin: Springer.

Miller, D T, 1975, "The Effect of Dialect and Ethnicity on Communicator Effectiveness", Speech Monographs 42, 68-74.

Miller, G A, 1951, Language and Communication, New York: McGraw-Hill.

Miller, G A, Heise, G A and Lichten, W, 1951, "The Intelligibility of Speech as a Function of the Context of the Test Materials", Journal of Experimental Psychology 41, 329-335.

Miller, G A and Friedman, E A, 1957, "The Reconstruction of Mutilated English Texts", Information and Control 1, 38-55.

Miller, G A and Isard, S, 1963, "Some Perceptual Consequences of Linguistic Rules", Journal of Verbal Learning and Verbal Behavior 2, 217-28.

Moore, T E, 1972, "Speeded Recognition of Ungrammaticality", Journal of Verbal Learning and Verbal Behavior 11, 550-60.

Morrison, S, 1955, "Measuring the Severity of Articulation Defectiveness", Journal of Speech and Hearing Disorders 20, 347-51.

Nas, G, 1975, "Determining the Communicative Value of Written Discourse Produced by L2 Learners: Progress Report", Institute of Applied Linguistics, University of Utrecht.

Nash, R, 1972, "Phonemic and Prosodic Interference and Intelligibility",in A Rigault and R Charbonneau, eds, Proceedings of the 7th International Congress of Phonetic Sciences, The Hague: Mouton, 570-73.

Nickel, G, 1972, "Grundsätzliches zur Fehleranalyse und Fehlerbewertung", in G Nickel, ed, Fehlerkunde, Berlin: Cornelsen-Velhagen & Klasing, 8-24.

Nickel, G, 1973, "Aspects of Error Evaluation and Grading", in J Svartvik, ed, Errata, Lund: C W K Gleerup, 24-28.

Olsson, M., 1972, "Intelligibility", The GUME Project, No 12, Department of Educational Research, Gothenburg School of Education.

Olsson, M, 1973, "The Effects of Different Types of Errors in the Communication Situation", in J Svartvik, ed, Errata, Lund: C W K Gleerup, 153-60.

Page, E B and Paulus, D H, 1968, The Analysis of Essays by Computer, U S Department of Health, Education, and Welfare.

Påhlsson, C, 1972, The Northumbrian Burr, Lund: C W K Gleerup.

Palmer, L A, 1973, "A Preliminary Report on a Study of the Linguistic Correlates of Raters' Subjective Judgements of Non-Native English Speech",in R W Shuy and R W Fasold, eds, Language Attitudes: Current Trends and Prospects, Washington, D C: Georgetown University Press, 41-59.

Perrin, E H, 1954, "The Rating of Defective Speech by Trained and Untrained Observers", Journal of Speech and Hearing Disorders 19, 48-51.

Philp, A M, 1968, "Attitudes to Correctness in English: A Linguistic View of Language in Use", Programme in Linguistics and English Teaching, Paper No 6, London: Longman.

Pollack I and Pickett, J, 1964, "The Intelligibility of Excerpts from Conversation", Language and Speech 6, 165-171.

Prator, C H, Jr, 1957, Manual of American English Pronunciation, Rev ed, New York: Holt, Rinehart & Winston.

Preston, M S, 1963, "Evaluational Reactions to English, Canadian French, and European French Voices", Unpubl M A thesis, McGill University, Montreal.

Quirk, R and Svartvik, J, 1966, Investigating Linguistic Acceptability, The Hague: Mouton.

Quirk, R, Greenbaum, S, Leech, G and Svartvik, J, 1972, A Grammar of Contemporary English, London: Longman.

Robinson, P, 1973, "Testing the Second-Language Competence of Children and Adults", English Language Teaching 27, 190-99.

Rose, R G, 1973, "Linguist and Nonlinguist Agreement Concerning Surface Structures", Journal of General Psychology 89, 325-26.

Rosenberg, S and Jarvella, R J, 1970, "Semantic Integration and Sentence Perception", Journal of Verbal Learning and Verbal Behavior 9, 548-53.

Ryan, E B, 1973, "Subjective Reactions Toward Accented Speech", in R W Shuy and R W Fasold, eds, Language Attitudes: Current Trends and Prospects, Washington, D C: Georgetown University Press, 60-73.

Schwartz, D, Sparkman, J P and Deese, J, 1970, "The Process of Understanding and Judgements of Comprehensibility", Journal of Verbal Learning and Verbal Behavior 9, 87-93.

Shanon, B, 1973, "Interpretation of Ungrammatical Sentences", Journal of Verbal Learning and Verbal Behavior 12, 389-400.

Sherman, D and Moodie, C, 1957, "Four Psychological Scaling Methods Applied to Articulation Defectiveness", Journal of Speech and Hearing Disorders 22, 698-706.

Sherman, D and Silverman, F H, 1968, "Three Psychological Scaling Methods Applied to Language Development", Journal of Speech and Hearing Research 11, 837-41.

Shriner, T H, 1971, "Economically Deprived: Aspects of Language Skills", in L E Travis, ed, Handbook of Speech Pathology and Audiology, New York: Appleton-Century-Crofts, 1143-62.

Shuy, R W and Fasold R W, eds, 1973, Language Attitudes: Current Trends and Prospects, Washington, D C: Georgetown University Press.

Spencer, N J, 1973, "Differences Between Linguists and Non-Linguists in Intuitions of Grammaticality-Acceptability" Journal of Psycholinguistic Research 2, 83-98.

Stenström, A B, 1975, "Grammatical Errors in Teacher Trainees' Written Work", Swedish-English Contrastive Studies, No 7, Department of English, Lund University.

Steube, A, 1968, "Gradation der Grammatikalität", in R Růžička, ed, Probleme der strukturellen Grammatik und Semantik, Leipzig: Karl-Marx-Universität, 87-113.

Stolz, W S, 1969, "Some Experiments With Queer Sentences", Language and Speech 12, 203-19.

Strongman, K and Woosley, J, 1967, "Stereotyped Reactions to Regional Accents", British Journal of Social and Clinical Psychology 6, 164-67.

Stubelius, S, 1968, Engelsk fonetik, Stockholm: Almqvist & Wiksell.

Sturtevant, E H, 1947, An Introduction to Linguistic Science, New Haven: Yale University Press.

Svensson, S G, 1974, Prosody and Grammar in Speech Perception, Stockholm: Institute of Linguistics.

Wang, M D, 1970a, "Influence of Linguistic Structure on Comprehensibility and Recognition", Journal of Experimental Psychology 85, 83-89.

Wang, M D, 1970b, "The Role of Syntactic Complexity as a Determiner of Comprehensibility", Journal of Verbal Learning and Verbal Behavior 9, 398-404.

Van Riper, C, 1947, Speech Correction: Principles and Methods, 2nd ed, New York: Prentice-Hall.

Váradi, T, 1973, "Strategies of Target Language Learner Communication: Message-Adjustment", paper presented at the Sixth Conference of the Roumanian-English Linguistic Project in Timisoara, 28-29 May, 1973.

Weinreich, U, 1953, Languages in Contact - Findings and Problems, Publications of the Linguistic Circle of New York, No 1, New York.

Weinreich, U, Labov, W and Herzog, M I, 1968, "Empirical Foundations for a Theory of Language Change", in W P Lehmann and Y Malkiel, eds, Directions for Historical Linguistics, London & Austin: University of Texas Press, 95-188.

Wilson, W R and Gasek, G, 1975, "The Influence of Pre-Information on the Rating of Articulation", Journal of Communication Disorders 8, 15-22.

Wolff, H, 1959, "Intelligibility and Inter-Ethnic Attitudes", Anthropological Linguistics 1, 34-41.

Ziff, P, 1964, "On Understanding 'Understanding Utterances'", in J A Fodor and J J Katz, eds, The Structure of Language, Englewood Cliffs, N J: Prentice-Hall, 390-99.